Praise for *Stakes Is High*

"Mychal Denzel Smith's *Stakes Is High* is the book we need. It dismantles American lies and instead offers a truth that feels like fire. Smith moves from point to point with a brilliant agility founded on a deep understanding of our history. A truly spectacular book."
    —Nana Kwame Adjei-Brenyah, author of *Friday Black*

"A fresh, modern, thrilling call for humanity to come together as well as a brilliant investigation into what it means to be an American. *Stakes Is High* is required reading."
    —Jami Attenberg, author of *All This Could Be Yours*

"*Stakes Is High* is Mychal Denzel Smith's gift to us. With compassion and intelligence, he shows us what justice is meant to be in America."
    —Common

"Mychal Denzel Smith has written an emotional break-up letter with hope. In his meditations on the pillars of American life, Smith challenges us to accept our complicity in the systems that link our fortunes to our oppressions. It is elegantly written and lovingly argued."
    —Tressie McMillan Cottom, author of
    Thick: And Other Essays

"From one of our country's clearest truth-tellers comes this collection detailing why we've arrived at this current moment and how we can move beyond it. *Stakes Is High* confronts the inherent failures of the American dream, the dangers and delusions of American empire, and helps us imagine ourselves into a more just future."

—Lisa Ko, author of *The Leavers*

"*Stakes Is High* is a passionate, urgent book, a personal account of a contemporary New York political education, and a call to confront the emergency with clarity and truthfulness about the history that brought us here."

—Hari Kunzru, author of *White Tears*

"*Stakes Is High* is that rare book written before the pandemic that predicts the American response to the pandemic and also provides a soulful, rigorous way out of the destruction. Mychal Denzel Smith is the rarest of tenacious writers who remind us that the only way into a dignified free future is backwards. And our refusal to go walk back together makes the stakes highest for the most vulnerable children of tomorrow."

—Kiese Laymon, author of *Heavy: An American Memoir*

"Nuanced, intimate, and sharp in its view of America's history and present, Mychal Denzel Smith's *Stakes Is High* offers a clear-eyed view of this nation's inequities, shortcomings, and self-deceptions. It's a beautifully written, timely, and illuminating book."

—Rebecca Traister, author of *Good and Mad: The Revolutionary Power of Women's Anger*

"With searing vision and unwavering clarity, Mychal Denzel Smith dismantles our most enduring myths and dangerous national illusions. His argument is personal, intimate. It calls on us, line by line, to do the hard work of truthful living: to hold past and present, love and criticism, up in equal measure. *Stakes Is High* will undoubtedly prove to be one of the most important works of the decade; as social critique, as personal essay, as a master class in language. Keep it within arm's length; you'll be reaching for it long after you've read the last line."

    —Téa Obreht, author of *Inland*

"I want this book in the hands of everyone it would affect, which is to say, those with power and those lacking power; those of every race and ethnicity who are affected by the United States government; those who have hope, those who do not, and those who are somewhere in between. Smith writes with urgency and brilliance, honing prose to a fine glimmer as he demonstrates, again and again, life after the American Dream."

    —Esmé Weijun Wang, author of
    The Collected Schizophrenias

"[Smith] is sharply self-aware, and he would seem to expect his reader to approach his fine-honed argument with the same seriousness. Doing so is well worth the effort. An urgent and provocative work that deserves the broadest possible audience."

    —*Kirkus*, Starred Review

"Smith addresses familiar topics through a fresh lens in these searing essays. . . . Infused with righteous indignation and astute observation, this is a must-read progressive polemic."

—*Publishers Weekly*, Starred Review

STAKES IS HIGH

STAKES IS HIGH

Life After the American Dream

MYCHAL DENZEL SMITH

BOLD TYPE BOOKS
New York

Bold Type Books
116 East 16th Street, 8th Floor, New York, NY 10003
www.boldtypebooks.org
@BoldTypeBooks

Printed in the United States of America

First Edition: September 2020

Published by Bold Type Books, an imprint of Perseus Books, LLC, a subsidiary of Hachette Book Group, Inc. Bold Type Books is a co-publishing venture of the Type Media Center and Perseus Books.

A portion of the text from Part 1 appeared on September 12, 2018, in the *Guardian*, with the title "Colin Kaepernick's Protest Might Be Unpatriotic. And That's Just Fine."

A portion of the text from Part 2 appeared on June 5, 2018, in the *New Republic*, with the title "Rough Justice."

A portion of the text from Part 2 appeared on September 11, 2017, in the *New Republic*, with the title "What Liberals Get Wrong About Identity Politics."

The Hachette Speakers Bureau provides a wide range of authors for speaking events. To find out more, go to www.hachettespeakersbureau.com or call (866) 376-6591.

The publisher is not responsible for websites (or their content) that are not owned by the publisher.

Print book interior design by Trish Wilkinson

Library of Congress Cataloging-in-Publication Data
Names: Smith, Mychal Denzel, 1986– author.
Title: Stakes is high : life after the American dream / Mychal Denzel Smith.
Description: First edition. | New York : Bold Type Books, [2020]
Identifiers: LCCN 2020001915 | ISBN 9781568588735 (hardcover) | ISBN 9781568588728 (ebook)
Subjects: LCSH: Equality—United States. | Prisons—United States. | Civil rights—United States. | Police misconduct—United States. | Discrimination in criminal justice administration—United States.
Classification: LCC HM821 .S58 2020 | DDC 973.933—dc23
LC record available at https://lccn.loc.gov/2020001915
ISBNs: 978-1-56858-873-5 (hardcover), 978-1-56858-872-8 (e-book)

LSC-C

10 9 8 7 6 5 4 3 2 1

For Gil Scott-Heron and Shirley Chisholm—
I don't know if you two ever met in life, but I'm glad
you met here and provided the guidance I needed.

For Dr. Lloren A. Foster—
I hope you got to read the first one before you left.
I hope you knew that I listened.

Contents

THE FORETHOUGHT

I keep thinking/the only city left/is outer space.
—MORGAN PARKER,
"SLOUCHING TOWARD BEYONCÉ"

What I was prepared to say the night of November 8, 2016—I'd been asked to appear as part of *Democracy Now!*'s election night coverage—was that the election of Hillary Clinton should be celebrated for what it is and acknowledged for what it isn't. We had eight years of the first black president to learn that representational progress, while important, does not necessarily translate to material progress, and it is that experience that should guide us in assessing the meaning of Clinton's triumph in becoming the first woman elected president of the United States, as well as how we strategize for pushing her administration moving forward. It is imperative—again, this is all what I had planned to say that night—to acknowledge that the rise of movements such as Occupy, Black Lives Matter, and the Dreamers illuminated the need to organize around the ongoing, structural problems that persist regardless of the political party in power at any given moment, but especially when it is the party trading on a message of progressivism. It must be possible to note a welcome change in the possibilities for marginalized people while also remaining skeptical of a system of governance that creates and maintains the conditions for their marginalization.

As you well know, reader, I didn't have the opportunity to say any of this. I can only present these thoughts to you now as things I once felt applied to a future I assumed would come to pass. I didn't plan for any other outcome, as I rehearsed these thoughts in my head over the course of the six-hour flight from New York City to San Francisco. I would be in town for a few days touring with Pop-Up Magazine, a "live magazine created for a stage, a screen, and a live audience," as its website puts it. I would be reading a short essay I wrote about sneakers, style, resistance, and activism. I had agonized over it for a few weeks, and now it feels too small to even mention.

The vibe on Twitter when my plane landed, at around 11:00 p.m. East Coast time, was markedly different from earlier in the day before I took off, when it seemed that thousands of liberal white women were posting selfies sporting Clinton-esque pantsuits at the polls. Fear had not yet settled in, but doubt was creeping. On the way to my hotel, assured optimism turned toward desperate pleading. By the time I was at the studio, it was full-on dread. The black woman who drove me there, with the radio feeding us real-time results, said all she could do was pray. She let me out of the car and hoped for my safety. I returned the wish.

When it was time for me to go on air, no networks could call it, but we all knew, even if some of us were refusing to be honest with ourselves.

What I ended up saying to Amy Goodman when she asked my thoughts about what we were seeing unfold that night was: "After eight years of the first black president . . . we have now elected a man who ran an explicitly racist campaign. That is not accidental. This is American history playing out before us. Whatever moments there are of progress, there is a backlash, there is a retrenchment, and white supremacy does what it can to protect itself. This is like the end of Reconstruction. . . . What we are witnessing is not some abnormality."

I was wearing a sweatshirt with the words "Catalyst for Change Shirley Chisholm for President '72" on it. I wondered to myself how things were going in the timeline in which Chisholm had won that election. I spent the rest of the night drinking with a friend, both of us sobbing as it was called in Wisconsin.

Two days after Trump won, I was in Oakland and found myself standing across the street from the building that was meant to be the next Uber headquarters (supposedly a sign of progress and revitalization), watching as images of the president-elect were projected onto its unfinished white siding. If I were a different kind of writer, this might be the point where my dystopian novel begins. But I've never had a flair for fiction and can only say to you, forlorn, that this dystopian vision was all too real.

Three days later, in a hotel room in Chicago, I was alone and listening to A Tribe Called Quest's new, and last, album, saddened again as I thought about the passing of Phife Dawg, hype to hear what hip-hop's greatest group would provide as its final offering. I was ready to declare it a classic as soon as I heard the hook for the first track, "The Space Program," which goes: *There ain't a space program for niggas/yeah, you stuck here, nigga.* Now, when my mind calls up the memory from Oakland, it fills in the silence left between police sirens with these lyrics. Because "here" is wherever I am—wherever we are.

Whether we are talking about Oakland, where forty years apart the police killed Lil' Bobby Hutton and Oscar Grant with plenty more in between, or

Chicago, where they closed forty-nine public schools in one cruel swoop, or New York City, where I now call home and where, for the first few years I lived there, I perhaps knew best from the vantage point of a protest, we are always "here" because there is no "there" where our destruction has not been carefully planned. There is no place where we have not been marked as other, where our otherness has not been used to justify our exploitation, and where our lives have not been defined by the limitations placed on them by whiteness.

You stuck here, nigga.

In the run-up to November 8, 2016, I heard good liberal white folks promise (or maybe they thought of it as a threat?) to move to Canada in the event that Trump won. I would nod politely and think to myself, *How quaint, yet another move they plan to hijack from black people.* But it must be nice to know there is a place you can go where you will be free. The police create niggers in Canada the same as they do here. I wonder if any of the good liberal white folks thought of any ideas for where *we* could go to escape.

Of course not. It has never truly been their concern. The good liberal white folks hardly even acknowledge that we have any cause for concern until one of us throws a trash can through a window, or flips over a car, or lights a gas station on fire. Only then do they seem to care, but not so much about us or the conditions that produced such anger, but more so about chastising our inability to be civil. The good liberal white folks tell us there is a resolution to our grievances that can only be achieved if we are willing to put aside our anger, frustration, pain, grief, and despair, and trade them for . . . what, exactly, isn't clear. Neither the emotions nor the facts of our condition persuade many of them that our lives are worth saving, so I remain unsure, and increasingly uninterested, in determining what will. No matter the method we choose to fight back, they are ready to chastise us. Our op-eds are too angry, our organizations too militant, our political demands too divisive, our votes wasted. Then they call our rebellions "riots" and ask why we tear down our own neighborhoods and I think what they really mean to say is don't mess it up any further before we have a chance to take it from you.

The irony is that after November 8, 2016, the good liberal white folks got good and mad and they had no idea how to go about being mad. Their "resistance" marches have proudly boasted their lack of disruption, while any conservative with even a tepid critique of the Trump administration has been branded a hero. They are, these resistance liberals, for the first time legitimately frightened of what the present and future hold for them, and they are not sure where to turn. They have since been in mourning for the loss of their America, where it was promised that hard work and determination would grant upon anyone who desired it the opportunity for a better life. This America has always been a fiction, and had they bothered to listen to us, to the pain they have always readily dismissed as misplaced rage, they would have known this was coming. Trump was inevitable and the evidence of his rise was sitting right there.

I don't intend to be a hypocrite and pretend I had this insight before the election. Sure, I read Trump as a backlash to the movements that threatened to push the country's aggrieved white men from their self-constructed pedestals. He spoke the language they had longed for—no longer coded in its hostility, but forthright in its provocation. I knew they were swinging desperately, hoping to land one last blow to keep them in a fight that they felt slipping away from them.

What I chose to believe, however, is that this is a nation so committed to its self-delusion that it wouldn't dare, in 2016, elect a true representative of its underlying ideology to its most cherished ceremonial perch. The days of acceptable public bigotry were supposed to be over.

I find myself, and many others, saying things like this from time to time, indignant over the fact that something objectionable from the past persists in the present, as if there had been some previously agreed-upon expiration date on injustice. But what it reveals is that even those of us with a healthy understanding of what created this nation also share in shaping its fiction. There is a part of us that wants to believe the good of America can outlast the bad.

If I am being more honest than this country has taught me to be, that is precisely why I moved to New York City. I was raised in Virginia, below the Mason-Dixon Line, which has always lived in the American imagination as the line of demarcation between the civilized and the non. I wanted out for fear of suffocation, that the ghosts of that land would swallow my dreams. From my youth I bought into the notion of the backward South, and so I romanticized New York as a place where creative minds flourish with relatively little interference from the history I hoped to escape. New York City would be the place where I would find like-minded rebels, sophisticated thinkers, off-kilter but fascinating weirdos, and the thing I sorely lacked my whole life in Virginia: belonging.

"It can destroy an individual," E. B. White wrote of New York, "or it can fulfill him, depending a good deal on luck. No one should come to New York to live unless he is willing to be lucky."

I have been lucky enough. In New York City I have found community, friendship, and love in abundance. But I have also found in this place a home where every day I am terrified. I am constantly on guard because I know my survival depends on such vigilance. If I were to fully relax, I fear, I would leave myself vulnerable to the destruction New York can so breezily ignite.

It's the kind of place that turns standing outside the building where you live into forty-one shots from police, as happened to Amadou Diallo in 1999 (nineteen of those hit him). That history is never idle; it pulses through every interaction I have here, as it did when I saw a "Make America Great Again" hat in the wild for the first and, to date, only time. It was the day after the Electoral College officially made Donald Trump the forty-fifth president of the United States. The unsightly red hats aren't a staple of New York City's ostensibly liberal streetwear—primarily feminist T-shirts and *New Yorker* tote bags. But there are pockets of Trump supporters, mostly concentrated in Staten Island, Queens, and parts of Brooklyn I never visit.

When I first moved to New York, I lived in Bushwick, a neighborhood largely populated by working-class Puerto Ricans and Dominicans whose accents range from first-generation immigrant to native New Yorker. There is, also, a creeping white hipster presence that was priced out of its former playground, Williamsburg. Now, I live in Flatbush—or at least you call it Flatbush if you've lived there since it was known as "The Jungle." These days you may call it Prospect Lefferts Gardens, as that name finds itself covering more and more territory beyond its original scope, a bit of real-estate trickery meant to dissociate a place from its reputation and assuage the fears of prospective residents. My new neighbors are still working-class people, still immigrants, but here they come from Jamaica and Trinidad. It is a neighborhood in the early stages of gentrification. The barbershops, nail salons, sneaker stores, and jerk-chicken spots haven't disappeared, but more than a handful of bars have cropped up, anticipating the demographic shift. The longtime residents are not oblivious to what is happening. No new construction goes unremarked upon, as luxury apartments are fully constructed almost overnight, right next to subsidized housing. I overheard a conversation between two people in the lobby of my building on my way out one day. They were having trouble renewing their leases. "They tryna push all the niggas out," one said to the other.

And yet, not one of the new residents is made to feel unwelcome. The mail lady greets the new white tenants the same as she does the more familiar black ones. The kids on the stoop across the street hold the door open for white dudes in cargo shorts carrying moving boxes. The brothers playing chess and politicking outside the laundromat greet white joggers with a healthy "Good morning." White people with only two items at the grocery store are instructed to jump in front of the woman with a cart full of groceries. Black and white addicts are served by the dope boys with the same standard of customer service. The black homeless beg black and white passersby alike for change and then apologize for their presence.

There is an abundance of evidence of black people's humanity here, and no one who matters is around to record it. Watching black folks perform daily kindnesses for the people meant to replace them is difficult to stomach.

For now, Flatbush a.k.a. Prospect Lefferts Gardens is a place that this white woman wearing the "Make America Great Again" hat will pass through. The Q train we shared took her, in all likelihood, to one of those neighborhoods where her red hat serves as a victory flag. She never had to consider what effect the message it carries might have on her neighbors directly north of her. She, perhaps, has never considered them as neighbors.

At the time, I was reading John Edgar Wideman's latest book, *Writing to Save a Life*, about the life and death of Louis Till, the father of Emmett Till. I wondered if, for her, the America that hat was referring to is the same America that, as punishment for charges of domestic violence, gave Till the choice between serving time in prison or time in the military during World War II, and when he chose the latter, sent him off to Italy, where he was convicted of raping and murdering two Italian women based on little to no evidence (a crime he didn't need to travel all the way to Italy to be accused of in 1940s America), and then hanged him. Or perhaps her red hat wants to take us back to the America of the younger Till, lynched in Money, Mississippi, in 1955 after being accused of whistling at and making sexual advances toward a white woman, who only recently admitted to fabricating parts of the story that led to Till's brutal death.

She did not, to my eyes, look old enough to remember either of these Americas, so perhaps she was pining for the days of the previous presidential candidate whose campaign slogan promised, "Let's Make America Great Again." Perhaps she was nostalgic for the nation of Yusef Hawkins, the sixteen-year-old black teenager killed by a mob of white teens in Bensonhurst in 1989. I never asked. Forgetting which America I live in is not a luxury that I can afford—it has always been the one where it is unsafe to exist in a black body and to challenge white authority, real or imagined.

And what a luxury it must be for this woman to be able to retreat to another America. Preserved in her mind is a country, one of prosperity and promise, where she feels protected. Her pristine America is under attack—by Mexicans, terrorists, takers of every hue—and her faith in the old America can only be restored via the bombast of an aging celebrity millionaire.

This is what her hat said to me, and she seemed not to care. She never looked my way, never looked beyond herself. She took her defiant victory lap through the other America, filled with people who have struggled mightily to realize the promise of this country. By rent or by force, landlords or ICE, their removal will mean that this woman can have the America tucked away in her mind returned to her.

It's not that I envy her vision of America. I would never hope to be so deluded. I envy the power of her narrative imagination. She has conjured an America, someplace in history, that is "great," and so many people are convinced of its existence that they create greater suffering in the present for people who stand to gain nothing from this imaginary restoration.

"The tradition of the oppressed teaches us that the 'state of emergency' in which we live is not the exception but the rule," philosopher Walter Benjamin wrote in *On the Concept of History* in 1940, and it endures. The nation finds itself in crisis, fretting over what comes next, debating what temporary measures can be taken to bring back normality even as it slips further away. But normal is no solution for those who never existed in normal's good graces. There are those of us who can retreat to a fantastical America, and those of us who are always here—stuck.

We need not be. There is a future that is not as grim as our past. But it is a future that depends on a bravery this country has never exhibited. It requires excess honesty and a radical retelling of who America has been. It will mean letting go of our myths and fashioning new selves based around principles we have thus far found difficult to live up to. We will have to relinquish old dreams and replace them with ones that meet the challenges we now face.

We will have to do it quickly.

PART 1

DELUSIONS

It was beautiful. Flames seemed to leap as high as the tenement roof. The row of brownstones across the street, reflecting the fire, was a shimmering red wall. The sky was a great red curtain. And from all over the city, we could hear the clanging of fire engines. Our bonfire never got out of hand but a lot of others did on election night.

Grandpa enjoyed the sight as much as I did, and he was flattered when I left the rest of the boys to come up to share it with him. He pulled his chair closer to the window and lit the butt of his Tammany stogie. "Ah, we are lucky to be in America," he said in German, taking a deep drag on the cigar he got for voting illegally and lifting his head to watch the shooting flames. "Ah, yes! This is a true democracy."

I had no idea what Grandpa was talking about, but he was a man of great faith and whatever he said was the truth.

—HARPO MARX,
HARPO SPEAKS . . . ABOUT NEW YORK

A nd then there is Donald Trump himself, who I am loath to write about but cannot avoid. He is as contemptible a figure as has ever existed, a receptacle for all the worst aspects of human expression. He suffers a lack of curiosity, compassion, and self-awareness, while over-indexing on bluster, dishonesty, and greed. All this is before you get to his proud racism and xenophobia, vile and violent misogyny, queer antagonism, enthusiastic militarism, and transphobia. Still, he became president.

For liberals shocked and outraged by the election results of 2016, it became popular, when speaking of Trump, to dismissively refer to him as "not my president" or, as an insult to a conversation partner, "your president." It's a rhetorical move with little consequence, but one that allows the speaker a perceived moral high ground: they are not responsible for the current state of affairs because this president does not belong to them. Whatever personal solace is achieved through this, however, is not matched with any real-world provocation—it simply doesn't matter if you claim him as *your* president or not, he remains *the* president.

I suppose I shouldn't begrudge people their small acts of sanity preservation; we all desperately need such acts in whatever form they may take. But this one in particular reveals a deeper problem with Americans and our relationship to the presidency. We do silly things such as vote based on the vaguely defined characteristic of likability, which produces ridiculous photos of politicians eating fried foods and drinking large beers, all because we want to feel that "our" president is someone who is like us in the ways that matter least to the function of the office.

Worse, though, is the sense that in choosing the "correct" person for president, one has fulfilled their democratic duties, and in the event the "correct" person loses, taking the brave moral stance of personally distancing yourself from the "wrong" choice—not *my* president—places you within an impenetrable cloak of righteousness. It is meant to signal that you are not yourself implicated in the worst of this presidency, and therefore cannot be tasked with doing much else to fend off the atrocities.

At the heart of the problem here is that the American presidency holds too much power, but not enough of the kind we imagine. When casting our ballot, we like to think of ourselves as steering the country in the proper direction, politically, socially, morally, and so on. The presidency, and therefore the person who becomes president, is assumed to represent the totality of our values, which is why those who voted against Trump would like to view him as an aberration, as a deviation from the American project.

The president is meant to be a part of an idealized, nearly apolitical American monoculture in which we all share. It is why we are implored to "respect the office" even when we disagree with the occupant, and why the president is expected to "put country first" while admonishing others to do the same. The president is regarded as both the leader and ultimate symbol of our nation, and as such is supposed to embody our mythical selves, not our reality. He is a uniter, not a divider. He is beyond the petty politics of the day.

What Americans who fret over "growing" divisions would like to believe is that we are all united by the idea of being Americans—that it holds the same meaning for each of us equally. And the only threat to this common identity are demagogues who accrue power by exploiting false ideas of difference. In order for this to be true, America must be something other than its people. Or its people must be something other than its politics. There must be an American monoculture to which we all belong, unsullied by the political divisions that upset the myth. This is an "all-American" culture that celebrates Thanksgiving, highways, Mickey Mouse, blue jeans, John Hancock, *Star Wars*, Coca-Cola, Frank Sinatra, Motown, hot dogs, World War II, James Dean, Jell-O, Kansas, Yankees/Red Sox, Ohio State/Michigan, Lakers/ Celtics, cowboys, "Give me liberty, or give me death!," Elvis Presley, oak trees, Superman, pumpkin pie, Budweiser, pickup trucks, Oprah, Monopoly, Jackie Kennedy, Valley Forge, 9/11, McDonald's, corn, the Super Bowl, golden retrievers, Babe Ruth, *Thriller*, red, white, and blue.

Part of the American delusion is to pretend that these cultural touchstones sprang forth independent of any ideology or agenda. This is not how people, politics, culture, or nations work. Babe Ruth is as much a symbol for the possibilities of whiteness under a system of segregation as he is some all-American beacon of greatness. Highways represent the possibility of travel, the open road, and freedom to those whose movement has never been restricted, or whose homes and communities were not destroyed in order to build these roads. Mickey Mouse has simultaneously delighted children and been the exemplar of corporate lobbying for copyright, trademark, and licensing laws. Thanksgiving is simply indefensible. Monopoly has no ideology if you think a game, so far from its socialist roots, in which the winner's goal is to own the most property and generate profit by driving up rent is nonideological.

Pickup trucks and oak trees are apolitical only if no one you have ever loved has had their body dragged behind one or hanged from the other.

The people of this country have never truly been united, beyond the framework of federalism. Even after the revolution that won independence from Britain, the former colonies had no desire for a singular national identity, as the Articles of Confederation created a weak central government that would ensure state sovereignty. Only another rebellion, led by Daniel Shays, which attempted to seize federal weaponry and overthrow the government, could serve as a catalyst for a unification project (funny what gets called a rebellion and what else is referred to as a riot).

"No one can say when the unwinding began—when the coil that held Americans together in its secure and sometimes stifling grip first gave way," journalist George Packer writes in his book *The Unwinding*. "The unwinding is nothing new. There have been unwindings every generation or two. . . . Each decline brought renewal, each implosion released energy, out of each unwinding came a new cohesion." Except this cohesion has never existed. To pretend otherwise is to acknowledge only one American experience from a single American perspective. Or else it is to pretend that the fissures underlying American life only matter when they disrupt the routine of those in power. It must hold, then, that the Civil War was the division, but not the preceding years of a system of slavery, or the bricks thrown at Stonewall were the point of division, not the queerphobic laws and police violence that existed long before that moment.

Perhaps what is so discomfiting for some is that Donald Trump is all too American. He is the American id, rather than a reflection of the myth. He does not make everyone feel better about themselves. There is no claim to moral superiority by association. He is deeply incurious. Arrogant. Convinced of his own importance. Dismissive of that which disputes his preferred narrative. A bully. Power hungry. Insufferable. Image obsessed. Indifferent to the suffering of others.

Donald Trump so undermines the idea of the president as agnostic leader that George W. Bush has come back around as a shining example of it. The scandals of the Trump White House move with such rapidity that nostalgia has set in for when they appeared only every few months. Trump has been so openly bigoted toward Muslims that Bush quotes about respecting Islam—absented the context of his all-out assault on majority Muslim countries—garner retroactive praise. Trump lies so much in service of himself that Bush's lies in service of empire are noble by comparison.

You can indulge this delusion if you don't live in Iraq or New Orleans. Or if you didn't lose your home because of predatory lending and treacherous Wall Street gambling. Then Bush can be your cuddly grandpa.

But what this nostalgia tells me is not that Americans forget too easily. "We are the United States of Amnesia, we learn nothing because we remember nothing," Gore Vidal famously said, but this is only partially true. He neglected that the delusion is intentional. The preamble to our Constitution starts, "We the People of the United States, in Order to form a more perfect Union . . . " and it has been interpreted as an excuse for America's shortcomings. We are not perfect, but seek to be "more perfect." Our faults are not American, only the progress—ending slavery is American, the institution itself was not. Extending the vote to white women via constitutional amendment is American, denying them the vote for more than a century of the nation's existence was not. For the myth to hold, we can only ever view America as the sum of its best parts.

Trump is a reminder of the ugliness we pretend only exists at the margins. The margins are much wider than some want to accept. To the extent that he has any ideas, they are those that have animated the Republican Party since at least the days of Nixon (ideas, it should be noted, that the Democratic Party has been all too happy to treat as legitimate, in the name of bipartisanship, which has been treated as another depoliticized American product). He is simply less polished than his predecessors, and purposefully so. Years of coded language have left the aggrieved white men who make up the Republican Party's base anxious about whether or not they have been heard. Trump put it in plain language, risking the alienation of the finicky American moderate, but shoring up the support of those who wanted it made clear: this country belongs to them. Trump promised to deliver it.

His instruments of repression have been blunt; Trump has never met subtlety. The travel ban did not dance around its intention to target Muslims. The only border he is intent on "protecting" is the one where the brown people enter. He doesn't bother often with diplomatic-sounding doublespeak, opting instead for the classic approach of making the perceived enemy disappear.

He is less artful when attempting the former. Sitting in a room surrounded by friendly black faces for his inaugural Black History Month breakfast, Trump rattled off a list of notable black Americans, and when he mentioned Frederick Douglass, he noted that Douglass was an "example of someone who's done an amazing job and is getting recognized more and more." He was, rightfully, mocked for sounding as if he didn't know Douglass had been dead for 122 years, and not even being familiar enough with Douglass's work and legacy to know why he would merit celebration.

But Trump is not alone in butchering Douglass's legacy. Out in New York the same shit is going on. Walking from Morningside Heights to get across Central Park one morning, I passed the Frederick

Douglass Houses, where there is a placard with a well-known quote from Douglass, which reads: "If there is no struggle, there is no progress." I raged for the rest of my walk. Forget Trump's ignorance. Here was, perhaps, a greater danger. Because for as long as that sign has been there (the housing projects were finished and opened in 1965), the residents have had this cherry-picked, decontextualized quote greet them at their home, mocking the legacy of Douglass, using him as another tool to reprimand poor people.

A fuller version of that quote reads: "If there is no struggle, there is no progress. Those who profess to favor freedom, and yet depreciate agitation, are men who want crops without plowing up the ground. They want rain without thunder and lightning. They want the ocean without the awful roar of its many waters. This struggle may be a moral one; or it may be a physical one; or it may be both moral and physical; but it must be a struggle. Power concedes nothing without a demand. It never did and it never will."

Douglass was addressing the white moderate, ever concerned with order, insisting that the struggle to abolish slavery would require more than an appeal to moral correctness. There would come a need for confrontation, an unsettling of the peace, or else the silence would lead only to the preservation of the institution. Douglass's words were meant to urge action in the face of oppression.

Now, those same words appear, stripped of their meaning, in a neglected place. They no longer urge critical confrontation with the oppressor, but are projected as an admonishment to the poor, black residents of this housing project. Struggle, they say, and you will be rewarded later. But you must struggle. Accept this now, live a charmed life later. This, the placard says, is for your own good. Absent the proper context, the quote now carries with it a message reinforcing an individualistic, capitalist-endorsed vision of success. That it appears to come from a figure as revered as Douglass discourages the kind of collective political struggle that he made his life's work.

Perhaps Trump still doesn't know who Frederick Douglass was. That is a shame. But I'd rather he not know than to weaponize Douglass in service of state violence. I'd rather he remain incurious than to find new ways to fold Douglass into the American myth.

But the damage has already been done, the meaning of Douglass's life and work already stripped away. He is as American as the golden retriever. The most insidious and remarkable quality of American mythmaking is the ability to swallow up the lives of those who stood in open rebellion to the American project and turn them into obedient symbols of American exceptionalism.

But this makes sense when you consider what James Baldwin wrote in his 1961 profile of Rev. Dr. Martin Luther King Jr.: "The problem of Negro leadership in this country has always been extremely delicate, dangerous, and complex. The term itself becomes remarkably difficult to define, the moment one realizes that the real role of the Negro leader, in the eyes of the American Republic, was not to make the Negro a first-class citizen but to keep him content as a second-class one."

It is only logical, from the standpoint of the empire, to swallow up anything that may threaten its existence. Dissent is inevitable but need not be destructive. By co-opting the heroes of insurgence, the empire is able to bolster its constructed moral authority.

I refuse euphemism here to speak directly of America's status as an empire, because it cannot honestly be called anything but. We speak dryly of America's role as the world's police, as if that is not a limp way of saying empire. We unironically refer to ourselves as the "leader of the free world," when in a truly free world, the notion of a singular leader of said "free world" would be ridiculous. Moreover, if that leader was a nation that made up only 5 percent of the global population and imposed its will on other nations at the threat of military violence and devastating economic sanctions, a free people in a free world would call that nation an empire.

I can sense, as I write this, those vociferous critics of American empire chastising me for the use of "we" here. To cast a "we" in a country so bitterly defined by its divisions is, in some way, to do what I have just criticized, in that it presumes a kind of unity that does not actually exist. In that, I understand the objections.

What I hope for in naming a "we" here is not to flatten the American identity into one of homogenous, uncritical agreement, but to own my place within the system. It is one thing to name the empire, and another to consider yourself as a citizen of it. I am an American, fraught as that designation is, and not simply because I was born here, right in the nation's capital. Nor is it because the wealth of this nation was built by my ancestors' labor, though it is that too. America *is* my inheritance. But I want to own that I am a product of American thinking.

Much of my political identity has been shaped in direct opposition to this current impulse. "I'm not an American," Malcolm X said, "I'm one of twenty-two million black people who are the victims of Americanism." Malcolm believed, and so for a long time I did too, that the only people with a claim to an American identity are those who have enjoyed its privileges and been spared its ugliness.

What I have come to accept is that being a victim of Americanism and a product of it are not mutually exclusive. It is the inescapable course for those of us who are not white, male, cis, hetero, and wealthy. Even as we suffer under the boot of oppression, we are not immune to indoctrination into the American myth. We are brought up in the very institutions that are responsible for perpetuating the lie of meritocracy, and it begins to sound plausible. The promise of a free, equal, and just America in which your destiny is completely in your own control sounds wonderful, and because it hurts too much to think that your future is controlled by anything more than your own actions, it is easy to fall under this spell, the illusion of democracy and freedom. America barely knows what it means when it uses these terms; we suggest that they are themselves American concepts—if we invented them, we hardly need to define them. And for a victim of America, they would seem to offer recourse to the damage America has done. So, you believe. You believe, at times, against your better judgment. You believe because you want to survive.

But survival on these terms is compromised, to say the least, as it encourages us to leave the fundamental questions about the American system unasked. Instead, it requires us to embrace a vague notion of the American Dream onto which we can project our personal ambitions.

It is unsurprising, then, to hear even those who have been most abused and dispossessed by America hum along to this country's praise songs. Our sense of our future prosperity depends on the continued existence of an America able to support the belief in our individual successes.

We know, too, that we risk alienation and retribution if we condemn America too strongly. Jimmy Carter never lived down the "malaise speech," which should be more accurately remembered as an energy and environmental speech that, had we heeded its suggestions, would have stemmed the global catastrophe we now face with climate change, all because he dared to say Americans faced a "crisis of confidence."

Those hardly even qualify as harsh words, but to the American ear trained to hear their president speak only in glowing terms of the American people and their spirit, it was as if he had prayed aloud for their deaths. He failed to appeal to the American ego, to be a cheerleader for American exceptionalism. In his post-presidency, by virtue of his global humanitarian work, Carter has come back to some level of reverence, but his presidency is consistently ranked near the likes of Chester A. Arthur, who signed the Chinese Exclusion Act, and Herbert Hoover, who had shantytowns named in his dishonor.

As Americans we are eager, ravenous even, to believe the most flattering narratives about ourselves. They don't have to be true; the hand-wringing over the age of "alternative facts" rings hollow when the history we teach is built on them. Bemoaning the lack of truth from our elected officials suggests that Americans have never actually been concerned about "truth" as such. We have only ever cared that we are made to feel good about ourselves as Americans— we like our independence from the British, our defeat of fascism in Germany and Japan, our first man on the moon, our Cold War victory. Those parts of our history that do not straighten our backs are either ignored or distorted to the point that they would be unrecognizable to the people who lived through them.

"I wonder, do we lie about history to absolve ourselves of guilt?" novelist Ottessa Moshfegh writes in her essay "Coyotes, the Ultimate American Tricksters." Or is self-deception simply a psychological trick that enables us to live with unchecked moral pomposity and exceptionalism?" It's certainly some combination of the two, but the effect of this is that those who champion the lies are called patriots, while anyone who takes actual American history as its history is deemed a radical.

But I have no interest in being a patriot, nor do I wish to recast dissent as patriotism, because I am not concerned with the viability of "America." My concern is always for people. It happens that the people here, on this land, call ourselves Americans, and have constructed an identity around that name, therefore, any attempt to fashion a future beyond it must deal with this identity and the reasons we have attached ourselves to it. We are—through force, choice, or happenstance—Americans, and as such we share *something*. Where we often disagree is on what that something is and its significance.

Dr. King reached for those commonalities in his appeals to white Americans to end segregation and disenfranchisement. He pointed to the founding documents of this country, which professed a love for liberty, and asked not that white Americans change their values but that they live up to them. This did not make him popular—no matter his flattering words for the American project, he was still asking that a despised people be included—but it did position him as the more "reasonable" alternative to those who would take up arms and call for revolution.

Except it could not last. Years of this work took a toll on the man, and it also exposed him to the depths of the problem. He moved from laudatory to audaciously skeptical. It is perhaps what got him killed. Exactly one year to the day he was assassinated, Dr. King stood in Riverside Church, here in New York City, to deliver his most forceful denunciation of the Vietnam War. He had, for several years, been including critiques of the war in his speeches, though he had been careful to not step into territory that might upset his delicate relationship with the Johnson administration or alienate his followers who were primarily concerned with black civil rights at home. King came to understand that these issues not only intertwined but spoke to something corrosive in the soul of this country.

That day in Riverside, he said:

> The war in Vietnam is but a symptom of a far deeper malady within the American spirit, and if we ignore this sobering reality . . . we will find ourselves organizing "clergy and laymen concerned" committees for the next generation. They will be concerned about Guatemala and Peru. They will be concerned about Thailand and Cambodia. They will be concerned about Mozambique and South Africa. We will be marching for these and a dozen other names and attending rallies without end unless there is a significant and profound change in American life and policy. So such thoughts take us beyond Vietnam, but not beyond our calling as sons of the living God.

He could not have known to include Afghanistan and Iraq at the time. I'm sure he hoped his warning would be enough and no new names would ever need to be added, because he was guided by an immense faith that this country would rebuke the militarism that causes destruction and poverty abroad and turn those resources toward its citizens crushed by generations of exploitation. I am always writing things I hope will one day no longer be true.

I've only been to Riverside Church once. It is, in short, majestic. I gave up belief in the Christian, capital-g "God" long ago, but sitting in the pews at Riverside inside what feels in the moment like an untouchable tower, I considered that if God were to exist, only this church would be fitting as tribute. And I considered what it must have felt like to believe in the power of such a God, to choose someone like Dr. King to speak on God's behalf, and then listen to him speak of the erosion of the American spirit.

I was in Riverside for a program honoring Dr. King, on the occasion of the national holiday recognized in his name. It was hosted by acclaimed director Ryan Coogler and the activist organization he helped cofound, Blackout for Human Rights. The intention of the program was to reclaim Dr. King from the whitewashing his legacy has undergone, as the politicians and institutions that stood against his work in his life have come to embrace his symbolism in death. The hope is that by reclaiming Dr. King, unsticking him from the National Mall and the "I Have a Dream" speech, it would then be possible to appreciate the full breadth of his work as an activist and political philosopher, much of which was highly critical of the cornerstones of the American Dream. But this asks us to use the posthumous reverence for Dr. King to our advantage, as though we can play upon the current acceptance of Dr. King and think it would make his true message more palatable. The whitewashing was deliberate and began almost immediately upon his assassination. Just two years after his death there were unofficial remembrances of his birthday, where thousands of people stayed home from work. But two years before he was killed, 63 percent of Americans held a negative opinion of him. It serves the purpose of ensuring that his words and example cannot be used in any other fashion than those that serve American patriotism.

The holiday cemented this. It was not the intention of those who worked to have it recognized, but the job of implementing it was turned over to the kind of people who would only ever honor Dr. King begrudgingly. On November 2, 1983, Ronald Reagan signed into law the Martin Luther King Jr. federal holiday. For years after King was assassinated, activists and lawmakers pushed for this holiday to commemorate the life and legacy of perhaps, for what it's worth, the greatest man this country can lay claim to. They aren't to blame for what happened after they won. In signing the bill, Reagan said:

> Now our nation has decided to honor Dr. Martin Luther King Jr. by setting aside a day each year to remember him and the just cause he stood for. We've made historic strides since Rosa Parks refused to go to the back of the bus. As a democratic people, we can take pride in the knowledge that we Americans recognized a grave injustice and took action to correct it. And we should remember that in far too many countries, people like Dr. King never have the opportunity to speak out at all.

With that, he effectively defanged King.

Now, the existence of Dr. King is treated as an American triumph, as though it is better to have had Dr. King than to have had justice. Reagan, never an admirer of Dr. King or his cause, transformed the activist into a major character within the American fable. Dr. King's accomplishments were recast as those of the democratic American people—never mind that it was the bigotry and violence of the American people and the profound lack of democracy that made Dr. King's work necessary.

America has never been a democratic nation in any way other than its own proclamation as such. It fails even by its own flimsy standards of democracy, which don't account for any aspect of life outside of the voting booth. Still, having failed to allow the franchise to poor white men until Andrew Jackson, to black men until Ulysses S. Grant, to white women until Woodrow Wilson, to black people (for real this time) until Lyndon B. Johnson, and never really to indigenous people, America's claim to democracy, wherein the government receives its power from the consent of the governed through free and fair elections, is tenuous in the most generous reading. This is before you begin to account for the lack of democracy within the voting system itself, or stretch to include economic and civic life.

Dr. King fought for the rights of black people to be full participants in a democracy that had yet to be built. The power brokers who would have opposed him now use him to ensure the democracy he envisioned never comes to fruition. They adopted Dr. King as a historic cudgel, because you can make a dead man believe whatever you want.

"I suppose there's not a lot we can do about his iconic status," says philosopher Tommie Shelby in an interview with the *Point*. "But it's possible to show a world-historical figure like him due respect without treating him like an infallible oracle."

Dr. King himself warned against something like this. After the assassination of JFK, Dr. King wrote a brief essay for the journal *Transition*, in which he says: "It is not necessary to create myths and legends about John F. Kennedy. It would diminish him because the facts abundantly honor him. There is the danger that in abstract exaltation his memory will shine brightly for [a] time and then fade."

These are rational positions to take, which is why they are also shortsighted. It is not necessary to create myths and legends, and it would indeed be preferable to deal in history, if you are not the beneficiary of the world those myths and legends created. The myths serve a function, which is delimiting our imaginations and setting the parameters of what is considered possible. Dr. King's treatment as an "infallible oracle" is not laziness; his perceived infallibility is related to the message he has been chosen to deliver. Reduced to an apolitical dreamer, he can be a tool to divert energy away from forming structural solutions to inequality and injustice while spreading grade-school-level bromides in favor of kindness.

Any attempt at reclamation must understand his current usefulness to the system, but also that if the myth were to ever be deconstructed, and his usefulness abated, Dr. King would no longer carry the meaning that makes him, now, a beloved figure. Restoring his radical legacy would make him as unpopular in death as he was in life.

What, then, to do with Dr. King? We could let him go. We could stop quoting him as an authority, stop turning to him in times of distress, stop arguing with those who have never read his work, stop inviting celebration of his hollowed-out memory, stop making him the center of our political vision . . . stop making him a piece of it at all. At least for a time. At least long enough that when we return to him, he is no longer useful as a tool for the systems that killed him.

But how do you justify abandoning an icon? He is not a fashion trend that can be so easily discarded. Dr. King has been embraced as a new Founding Father. He has been stitched into the fabric of the American flag.

Which is precisely why he can be left behind. Attachment to the symbols of the myth leave us attached to the myth itself. The symbols uphold the ritual of lying to ourselves about the disconnect between the stated values of the nation and the reality carried out in our institutions. Disengaging with those symbols can begin the process of unraveling the myth.

This is what made Colin Kaepernick's national anthem protest, which he began during the 2016 NFL season, so powerful. "I am not going to stand up to show pride in a flag for a country that oppresses black people and people of color," Kaepernick said at the time when his protest was noticed by the press. "I'm going to continue to stand with the people that are being oppressed. . . . When there's significant change and I feel that flag represents what it's supposed to represent, and this country is representing people the way that it's supposed to, I'll stand," he said in a follow-up interview.

Such defiance did not go over well with those Americans whose reverence for the flag is directly tied to their reverence for the military, which they view as the singular force in ensuring America remains "free." Kaepernick stoked their ire because he refused to participate in the compulsory, militaristic patriotism ordered by the NFL while American institutions, represented by the flag and honored by the anthem, continued to carry out the violent repression of America's citizens. His protest dramatized the failure of the anthem's promise to carry over into its country's systems of governance. It was a much stronger rebuke than Carter's malaise.

Lost in the ensuing debate about whether or not the protest was respectful of the flag was the reason Kaepernick began the protest, which he stated many times over—the repeated police killings of black people, done with impunity. That this point fell away from the discourse understandably frustrated those who supported the protests, but it also led to a dilution of the protest's meaning. In defense of Kaepernick, supporters took to saying that he was not protesting the national anthem or the flag, though he very much was. They were not the reason for his protests, but they were the targets, precisely because of their symbolism. But in a futile attempt to win over those Americans stubbornly committed to perpetuating our national myths, ground was ceded to turn Kaepernick's protest into something more benign, even patriotic.

But patriotism is not a higher virtue than justice. Nor are they synonymous, which is what the kneeling protests, at their most potent, reminded us. Whether or not they were "American" in nature is inconsequential if we, as Americans, have failed to provide that term with meaning beyond the delusions we pass off as national treasures. If the flag is big enough to contain the diametrically opposed ideologies of the police who kill and the people who protest the killing, then the principles it is meant to stand in for are shot through with an inconsistency that cannot hold. It must come down on one side or the other. To be American must either be an embrace of freedom or an embrace of racist violence, because thus far attempting to straddle the hypocritical middle of these two has resulted only in pain, frustration, conflict, and death that is poised to continue indefinitely.

If I step back from the fire of this declaration of what America must do, I have to laugh at myself a bit. I don't believe I am wrong—the country certainly must embrace freedom, real freedom, for all its people if it cares at all to survive. But I wonder if survival is the goal. I sometimes think that a slow suicide may be the point. It is not easy to wear the crown. It means you are ever watchful for someone coming to take it away. Sometimes that fear means destroying yourself rather than letting anything change. But even the tension that produces, deep inside your tissue, would seem preferable to losing it when you fear being trampled by those you have kept underneath your own boot.

Author Norman Mailer, in writing about himself and his relationship to Muhammad Ali and the Black Power movement of the 1970s, wrote: "But his love affair with the Black soul, a sentimental orgy at best, had been given a drubbing through the seasons of Black Power. He no longer knew whether he loved Blacks or secretly disliked them, which had to be the dirtiest secret in his American life." Such confusion only breeds more contempt, as those in powerful and privileged positions feel simultaneously elated and threatened by the insurgence of their diminished subjects. They genuinely don't know what to do, until they imagine that they themselves may be subjected to the cruelty they have wrought. They must decide between their suicide and a return to the myth, though it is not always clear where the separation between the two lies.

At times, though, cracks start to show. It's hard to remember that Hillary Clinton actually received more votes than Donald Trump—around three million more. The majority of voters rejected Trump, or rather some sixty-five million voters rejected a version of the myth.

That is hard to remember since he became president anyway. His victory required explanation, as it did not fit either the inevitable narrative that had been built around Clinton or the progress narrative that has served as the core myth for America's sensible electorate. Alternately it became the fault of the economically anxious, the 53 percent of white women, non-voters, young people, third-party voters, and Russian hackers. Choose your scapegoat, choose your evidence, and repeat it until you felt it was true.

And there is something true in each of these explanations, though none get at the core truth that brought us to this moment: America always returns to itself. Trump won because we have not abolished the Electoral College, which was the idea of the slave owner James Madison, proposed to ensure that slaveholding states would not be outvoted by their non-slaveholding counterparts. Trump secured the nomination because at least one major American political party has always explicitly or implicitly endorsed white supremacy as the ruling ideology. The white supremacist political party chose a white supremacist to represent it in the presidential election. An institution created for the protection of white supremacy installed that white supremacist into the nation's highest office. The system worked precisely as it was intended to.

And so the three million additional votes for Clinton are cold comfort. And should there be any comfort at all? It would be easy to draw hope from those three million votes, because if you wanted to (or, more correctly, if you needed to), you could take those votes to mean that we are a nation intent on bettering itself. Except flattering ourselves is part of how we ended up here. It's why all our so-called progress has been hollow. It's why the so-called progress is so easily undone.

Perhaps I am, again, being too harsh. Progress is progress. It certainly happens, and its benefits are felt. And progress is hard. Progress is wrestling concessions from the behemoth of systematized oppression.

The problem is when progress becomes its own ideology—that is, when advocacy for incrementalism is seen as the astute and preferred mode of political transformation. It is never easy to win, but progress is also never sufficient. Incremental change keeps the grinding forces of oppression—death—in place. Actively advocating for this position is a moral failure.

But progress is at least something concrete, something we can see, so we then become enamored with it. When we have done what is hard, we have convinced ourselves that hard is a synonym for revolutionary. We have changed this country in important ways, but the principles that formed it remain intact.

To our detriment, we allow the lie of what those principles are to govern us. So when a rupture point comes along, as it did with the 2016 election, it is easy to become nostalgic for a past that never existed but that fits the collective delusion of who we believe ourselves to be.

What we are—what America is—is a country so fearful of its biggest challenges that it would rather wither away under the leadership of committed liars than face the judgment of its own history. America is an empire built on cowardice.

It need not remain one. We need only listen when critical voices warn against the kind of thinking that produces empiric modes of violence. In March 1969, after becoming the first black woman elected to the US Congress, Shirley Chisholm delivered her first speech on the house floor. She spoke out against the Vietnam War, saying:

> We Americans have come to feel that it is our mission to make the world free. We believe that we are the good guys, everywhere, in Vietnam, in Latin America, wherever we go. We believe we are good guys at home, too. When the Kerner Commission

told white America what black America has always
known, that prejudice and hatred built the nation's
slums, maintains them and profits by them, white
America could not believe it. But it is true. Unless
we start to fight and defeat the enemies in our own
country, poverty and racism, and make our talk of
equality and opportunity ring true, we are exposed
in the eyes of the world as hypocrites when we talk
about making people free. . . . For this reason, I intend to vote "no" on every money bill that comes to
the floor of this House that provides any funds for
the Department of Defense. Any bill whatsoever,
until the time comes when our values and priorities
have been turned right-side up again, until the monstrous waste and the shocking profits in the defense
budget have been eliminated and our country starts
to use its strength, its tremendous resources, for
people and peace, not for profits and war.

There have always been voices willing to take on the
fragile American ego—at times, they have even managed to infiltrate the halls of power. At their most
critical and potent, they disabuse us of the notion
that America's foibles can be overlooked in favor of

a notion of our inherent goodness. They ask not that we consider how America, which has only ever existed as a project of white supremacist heteropatriarchal capitalism, can survive, but the more important question, once posed by Gil Scott-Heron: *Who will survive in America?*

PART 2

JUSTICE

This is something everyone already knows. A well-used city street is apt to be a safe street. A deserted city street is apt to be unsafe. But how does this work, really? . . . There must be eyes upon the street, eyes belonging to those we may call the natural proprietors of the street. The buildings on a street equipped to handle strangers and to insure the safety of both residents and strangers, must be oriented to the street. They cannot turn their backs or blank sides on it and leave it blind.

—JANE JACOBS, *THE DEATH AND LIFE*
OF GREAT AMERICAN CITIES

The limits of my language mean the limits of my world.

—LUDWIG WITTGENSTEIN,
TRACTATUS LOGICO-PHILOSOPHICUS

I know that where I live is the hood, and not only because I am in a part of Brooklyn where a substantial number of black people still live. Nor is it because for a solid month before the Fourth of July, my neighbors and I all play the game "gunshots or fireworks?" It is not the constant police presence, though that certainly helps with identifying it. I witnessed half a dozen police officers respond to one shoplifting call, and that was after the accused had already been handcuffed. But still this is not the telltale sign of the hood.

It is the trash. There is trash everywhere, always. There are nearly 8.5 million people living in New York City, and this does not include the tourists and bridge-and-tunnel folks who flow in and out on a daily basis. Of course there is an abundance of trash. But when I get off the train to walk to my therapist's office on the Upper East Side, a neighborhood devoid of any of the character that makes New York City appealing, I notice there is no trash on the street. More people live in this neighborhood than where I live; presumably they are creating more garbage, but their clean streets would suggest otherwise. Any casual observer might suggest that the people who live in my neighborhood—mostly poor, mostly black, mostly immigrant—take less pride in where they live. They throw their candy wrappers and used napkins, their half-emptied soda bottles and unfinished pizza, their Styrofoam to-go containers and paper receipts, on the ground because they don't care about keeping their sidewalks presentable and livable.

And this, the observer may argue, is because of a cultural deficiency (as though those monied white people on the Upper East Side don't also leave their cigarette butts on the ground, throw their water bottles every which way, leave discarded chicken bones on the sidewalk). They do not value this place, their home, because those values have not been inculcated by their surroundings. Some of these observations have been turned into academic studies that became the foundation for what we now call "broken windows policing," which claims that if such minor infractions are allowed to fester, they serve as the prelude to much larger, more serious crimes.

Little, if any, consideration is given to the fact that there are fewer public trash cans in my neighborhood.

On the walk from the train station to my therapist's office, there seems to be a trash can on every corner. They are fewer and farther between on the ten blocks from my local subway stop to the next one, on the always crowded, always bustling Flatbush Avenue.

The city could put more trash cans here, if it decided there was a need. If it were important to keep this neighborhood where mostly poor, mostly black, mostly immigrant people live as clean as the neighborhoods where mostly affluent, mostly white New Yorkers live and work and go to therapy. But then the city would also have to pay someone to collect that garbage from those cans. The city's elected officials would need to deem these residents worthy of that expense.

What these officials *have* deemed the hood worthy of is policing, and not because it is so much cheaper. Police are a costly public service, but it's the most readily available one here. There are undercover officers busting drug dealers. There are uniformed officers in patrol cars sitting on corners all day, all night. Sometimes they are standing next to huge, overpowering floodlights, warning the criminals off the street. Sometimes there are raids, ten to fifteen squad cars deep, where one to two people are arrested. The police are always on duty here. The people here do not lack for police, the way they do trash cans. There is enough money to keep the police here in my neighborhood. Always, there is enough will to keep the police in the hood.

The same casual observer, and they will likely be joined by others, may tell you that it is because there is so much crime in this hood. The people here are lawless, violent. The dope boys standing outside the bodega, quietly selling drugs and loudly shooting the shit, pose a threat to public safety.

And it's true, there is violence here, just as there is violence any place where the people are stripped of the means to build a meaningful life. The gunshots, though not as frequent as they may have once been, still ring out. Men threaten women with violence, women shout back their intentions to retaliate. The kids learn early to settle their petty disputes with slapboxing, which transitions smoothly into fistfights. The dope boys discuss their most recent brushes with death, while mourning those who weren't so lucky. Violence confers respect, the only currency that matters when the resources are scarce and competition for them breeds contempt. Violence is protection, or rather, it is itself a method of survival.

I know that I live in the hood because when I tell someone where I live, there is a good chance they will say, "Oh, that's over by the sketchy side of the park," and I'm left to wonder what, for them, makes my side of the park "sketchy." I see children Hula-Hooping and throwing footballs, hear the music of my parents' youth blasting in competition with the music of today's youth, see the smoky grills and packages of hamburger buns, and this all looks and feels warm and playful.

There are police, though, always more police. After all, the reason it is sketchy has little to do with what actually goes on there, but rather who is doing it. Blackness is itself the evidence of wrongdoing.

Those casual observers, who aren't always so casual—they begin to include academics, media professionals, policymakers, presidents—excuse the presence of the police here, and in other hoods like this one, because it is their position that in order to stop the violence of the hood you must impose the violence of the state. The police are meant, from this view, to protect the people from themselves, to enforce the discipline their culture lacks.

It requires a preposterous understanding of the police to view them as heroes. They have an efficient propaganda machine to ensure this rosy view of them survives. Different cities may refer to their police units as the "finest" or the "bravest." Serious-minded journalists report in their papers and magazines from the perspective of the police, allowing their version of events to stand as the unimpeachable truth. Lawmakers profusely thank them, as though the police have done them the personal favor of saving their lives every single day. Children are encouraged to imitate them and are applauded when they say they want to grow up to be them. Hollywood turns out movie after movie, show after show, where the police are living gods capable of mesmerizing stunts and crime solving through infallible wisdom, working-class grit, and compassion for the aggrieved.

This is all bullshit, and once anyone encounters a police officer doing their actual job, they know it is bullshit. Police patrol and harass. They reluctantly answer questions better suited for town visitor centers. They enforce traffic laws at their discretion, or to shore up municipal budgets through the imposition of exorbitant fines. They introduce the potential for violence in response to calls about loud music. They arrest people who have disobeyed them and then make up the charges later. They dismiss the stories of rape victims; they side with domestic abusers. They commit rape and domestic abuse at higher rates than the rest of the population. They quell rebellions. They arrest freedom fighters. They shoot and kill with impunity.

They do all these things because they have not strayed so far from their roots. The first modern police force—the London Metropolitan Police—was established by Sir Robert Peel in 1829. He developed his ideas about law and order, Alex S. Vitale writes in his book *The End of Policing,* when he was "managing the British colonial occupation of Ireland and seeking new forms of social control . . . in the face of growing insurrections, riots, and political uprisings." The "Peace Preservation Force" was meant to serve as a less expensive alternative to the British Army, which had previously been tasked with quelling Irish resistance. Appointed home secretary in 1822, Vitale writes, Peel would run the London Metropolitan Police along the same lines. Although the group claimed political neutrality, its main functions were "to protect property, quell riots, put down strikes and other industrial actions, and produce a disciplined industrial work force."

Boston adopted the London model in 1838, and New York established a formal police force in 1844. But well before then, cities in the southern United

States, such as New Orleans, Savannah, and Charleston, "had paid full-time officers who wore uniforms, were accountable to local civilian officials, and were connected to a broader criminal justice system," Vitale writes. These police officers were charged with preventing slave revolts. They had the authority to go onto private property to make sure enslaved people were not harboring weapons or conducting meetings, and they enforced laws against black literacy. Policing became the primary method of eliminating vices (gambling, prostitution, drugs, and alcohol under Prohibition) during the late nineteenth and early twentieth centuries (Theodore Roosevelt was recruited to become New York City Police Commissioner in 1895 with precisely this mandate, though, spoiler, he failed). Then in the 1960s, in response to the urban uprisings that erupted from black people's frustration in dealing with generations of poverty and social neglect (as well as constant police harassment), Los Angeles Police Department Inspector Daryl Gates conceived of the "Special Weapons Attack Team," or SWAT, a specially trained unit meant to be quickly deployed with heavy artillery capable of ending any uprising with overwhelming force (the acronym now stands for "Special Weapons and Tactics"). As the 1970s and '80s gave rise to the "War on Drugs," use of these SWAT units increased as the police became more of a paramilitary force, a transformation completed after the attacks of 9/11, when police were enlisted into so-called counter-terrorism measures, which have been little more than pretense for surveillance and harassment of Muslims.

The motto "to protect and to serve"—adopted by the LAPD in 1955 and later used by others around the country—has been a highly effective public relations tool, as it obscures the main function of their work, which since its inception has been to act in an adversarial manner toward already disenfranchised communities. "Police often think of themselves as soldiers in a battle with the public," Vitale writes, "rather than guardians of public safety." This has held true through the last century and up to the present: in the Memorial Day Massacre of 1937, in which the Chicago police killed ten protesters during a steelworkers' strike; in the raid of the Stonewall Inn in 1969; in the killing of Stephon Clark, a twenty-two-year-old black man whom the Sacramento police shot at twenty times on March 18, 2018, in his grandmother's backyard. No matter what other responsibilities police have assumed, they have consistently inflicted violence on the most marginalized people in society and maintained the economic, political, and social dominance of the ruling class.

When I say they have not strayed too far from these roots, I mean precisely that the main function of policing has not changed. It is still an institution built on the principle of using violence to ensure that people who are exploited by the ruling class are unable to assert any pressure on their oppressors. The perfunctory nod to "crime solving" has only opened the door for the police to use more aggressive tactics to strike greater fear in the hearts of the already afflicted.

But with the propaganda machine churning on, the police, and the governments that direct them, are able to get buy-in from the very people they are meant to police. The community hears the gunshots, sees the addicts wandering hopelessly and the dope boys pondering their next move, grows fearful that a shouting match will turn ugly quickly, and they have been taught by teachers, counselors, television, movies, and the police themselves that the cops can solve this problem. So they call.

There is no alternative. No one will even pay for them to have trash cans. How can a community deprived of the basics expect to receive the resources they need to no longer depend on police? They have, purposefully, been given nothing else. When they ask, they are told to wait; when they shout, they are told that it makes them undeserving. They are shamed for the ways they have survived. They are blamed when they don't survive.

The police are no solution, but they are, as it were, the final solution. It matters what you see as the problems in need of solving. Is it the people or the conditions? Is it blackness or anti-blackness? Is it poverty or the poor?

When people become problems to solve, it produces a callous indifference toward life. A lesson you learn fairly quickly while living in New York City and using public transportation is that if there is an empty subway car on an otherwise crowded train, you do not want to get in that subway car thinking you've somehow hacked the system. It only takes one or two times believing you've outsmarted all the other passengers to realize the smell of that empty car is so repulsive, no person can reasonably bear it for any amount of time. Except there likely is a person in that car, and that person has likely been homeless for some time. The subway car is their safest refuge. They have likely been riding for hours, having hustled their way on at last, winning a swipe from one of the hundreds of people who have passed them by. They finally have a place to rest, but it has been who knows how long since they have been able to avail themselves of a bathroom, because in New York City all the restrooms are for customers only, and you can't become a customer when you have no money. So they smell like the piss and shit that they've been unable to wipe from themselves, now caked up and causing other passengers to run away, leaving them further alienated from any sense of humanity and community. We, those of us lucky enough to have homes, make the choice to run away, to protect ourselves from the smell that rots and that we can begin to taste, and we warn others that they should do the same. And the person who is struggling to survive is left alone.

Only they won't be left alone for too long, because someone else who is even more uncaring will not tolerate it, will not simply choose another subway car. They will see it as their right to ride unencumbered by the sight and smell of this other person. They will call the police, who will arrest this person, and for a night or two they will have a place to sleep in a jail cell.

The police cannot solve poverty, joblessness, and the housing crisis—the actual culprits in the lives of the homeless. But if we've deemed the homeless, not poverty, the problem, then what the police *can* do is make them disappear. The major tools the police carry are handcuffs and guns; they can arrest or kill. The police can go forth and round up the homeless, then place them in cages. And to grant them the authority, local governments can criminalize the existence of the homeless: they can criminalize sleeping outside, or criminalize panhandling, which begins to look a lot like the criminalization of vagrancy as part of the Black Codes in the era that ended Reconstruction. And then, our local governments can fund a separate police force for the subway system to punish turnstile jumpers, arrest women selling churros, and clear out more homeless people, while neighborhood associations ensure no new homeless shelters get built near or in affluent neighborhoods. The streets remain the only place for them to call home.

I have never, and would never, call the police because the sight or smell of a homeless person offended me. It is such a cruel act. But I am guilty of scrunching my face, holding my nose, and running away from their smell on the train, as though the stench is so significantly worse than what the city carries day-to-day. Then I will attempt to assuage my guilt by giving cash to any person who has brought themselves to ask. Often they concoct stories, like the woman who told me she needed only two dollars because she had found a dress on sale, or make up starving children and spouses who are unable to fend for themselves (perhaps some of these are true), while forcefully denying any addictions to prove that they are "worthy" of my money, as if it should be any of my business what they do with the money after I have given it to them. If alcohol or more illicit drugs make them feel better while they live a life on the street, then so be it. I give what I can.

When I have it. I don't tend to carry much cash on me these days. Everything is digital now; I even borrow and lend money to friends through my phone. More businesses are going cashless, and this strikes me as a heartless move, one meant to preserve their establishments from being tainted by the mere presence of the poor (some cities are recognizing this and pushing to outlaw this practice, including New York City, which passed a ban on cashless businesses in January 2020). If you have spent all day on the street asking for money, gotten just enough to buy the minimum sustenance in loose change and guilt-laden bills, how damning it must feel to then be told your cash is not wanted. How depressing it must be to know your survival depends on the cash of cashless strangers who ignore you when they are unwilling or unable to give. Even when I can't give, I at least speak, at least say, "I'm sorry," at least acknowledge their presence so they know that someone sees them as human.

Giving, even a little, makes me momentarily feel better, knowing the person who now has a bit of cash may be able to eat something, or get whatever substance helps them cope. But getting too high on my own generosity would be a mistake, as it is as temporary a fix as when others make the choice to call the police. My dollar here, two dollars there, five when I'm a little more flush, do not begin to address what actually ails the poor and homeless, but the political will to say the real problem out loud barely exists. Lawmakers, and those who aspire to become them, will continue to send the police to arrest the poor because they respond to two groups, funders and voters, and the poor are neither.

New York has always been a gilded city, with extremes of wealth and poverty crammed next door to each other. The masters of capital are dependent on the labor of the impoverished to keep the city humming while they hoard wealth and push those very same workers to the outer edges of the boroughs, a crisis revealed to some during the COVID-19 pandemic. For the wealthy, even the sight of the poor ruins the allure that makes them want to call New York home.

America is loath to admit poverty exists here. Our official metric of poverty defines poor people out of existence, lumping even the most economically precarious into categories like working or middle class. American citizens do not want to believe themselves poor, as poverty is treated as moral failure in this country. The Dream tells us that we can achieve whatever it is we desire through hard work, but in reality we have financed that Dream through massive amounts of debt because there is no level of hard work that can purchase what the Dream has promised. As we struggle, we refuse to abandon the identity that lends credence to the Dream. We live on the edge of savage destitution and still call ourselves middle class because we are conditioned to believe that the poor exist as a product of their lack of ambition, cleverness, and ingenuity. We want to think ourselves clever and diligent and worthy. It would be a tremendous shame for the wealthiest nation in human history to admit that the wealth it has built came at a dreadful cost to the majority of people who live here. It would reveal the lie of the whole system.

Contrary to what personal finance charlatans would have us believe, poverty is not a mindset—it is the inevitable and necessary by-product of a system wherein life is only guaranteed to those who have wealth and wealth is distributed via ownership and not labor. Poverty is a capitalist's main resource, as it ensures there will always be a class of people to exploit.

I learned this lesson not from Karl Marx but from Iceberg Slim when I read the latter's memoir *Pimp*. Pimping (not sex work) is capitalism in its purest form: all the profits generated by labor end up in the hands of ownership/management that performed none of the labor. The workforce is viewed as dispensable, replaceable the moment they refuse to toe the line. Violence, both implicit and explicit, is central to regulating the worker: implicit violence lies in understanding that your livelihood can be threatened if you speak out of turn—you may lose your ability to provide for yourself (and whatever family you have) with food, clothes, and shelter; explicit violence is a last resort. The pimp must use his own hands. A legit capitalist can call upon the violence of the state to act in their stead.

But what Iceberg Slim stressed is that the key to the pimp's survival is presentation. His clothes are flashy, bright, overstated, and not by accident; he means to draw your eyes to him. His car is too big, his jewelry especially gaudy. His mouth moves a mile a minute. A pimp's greatest asset is his mouth because it is here that he is able to build an illusion. It's here that he sells you on his own success and how much success you can have with him. He imagines for you a life of riches, decadence, a life where all the things you ever dreamed up are possible. If only you follow his lead, trust in him, do exactly as he says, because he has a vision, and if everyone believes in that vision and works toward it, there is nothing but prosperity to be had.

The pimp, of course, assumes none of the actual risk—the bodily harm, legal threats, economic precarity. They assume responsibility for those working for them only to the extent that it impinges on their ability to earn. They themselves use the threat of violence, or termination, to ensure loyalty.

But they would prefer to seduce you. They would rather you believe that they have your best interests in mind as their own best interests, because violence only carries loyalty so far. If they can get you to care for them as you care for yourself, or your loved ones, they can make you feel indebted to them for much longer.

The capitalist promise is enticing. Work hard, see untold rewards. Dream as big as you can, you can have it all. Except it is impossible to fulfill if the direct result of your labor does not belong to you. If you cannot access the profits you have generated, you will only have promises and dreams to cling to. Those will carry you but only so far.

"A good pimp has to use great pressure," Iceberg Slim wrote. "It's always in the cards that one day that pressure will backfire. Then he will be the victim."

In the past decade, we have seen the pressure backfire and have finally come back to a place where capitalism is receiving a public hearing. At the beginning of the twentieth century, it was much more common to debate the merits of capitalism; socialists actually held political offices and exercised real power. But capital rallied through propaganda campaigns and military suppression of socialist uprisings abroad, and the threat of the Soviet bogeyman was able to excise from the public discourse any meaningful critiques of capitalism, and thus any real momentum in establishing democratic socialist governance. This also had the effect of separating movements that would otherwise have a natural kinship; the Red Scare, with its charges of anti-Americanism, was enough to turn black-led organizations away from any radical leftist leanings, as a key part of their strategy in advocating for black people's rights relied on playing up black people's Americanness, our belonging here, and the promise of the American Dream. Those who stood defiantly against this turn saw themselves marginalized; Paul Robeson's career was destroyed because he refused to denounce communism. Historian Manning Marable placed the turning point at the election of Harry Truman, who "privately viewed the blacks' goals of social and political equality with great contempt" but, in an effort to shore up his electoral victory over his Republican challenger Thomas Dewey, "immediately responded to blacks' interests by publicly calling for new civil rights legislation." This had the effect, Marable wrote in his book *Race, Reform, and Rebellion*, of silencing and isolating "black progressives for many years, and committed the NAACP and most middle-class black leaders to an alliance with Democratic presidents who did not usually share black workers' interests, except in ways which would promote their own needs at a given moment. Accommodation, anti-communism, and tacit allegiance to white liberals and labor bureaucrats became the principal tenets of black middle-class politics for the next decade."

But other factors have kept black political thinkers and organizations from allying with or incorporating socialist thought. There has been the sense that what liberation means is access to the same systems as white Americans; in other words, discrimination has been harmful insofar as it has denied black people the right to participation within capitalist enterprise, and opening up avenues by which black people could become full participants would be an adequate form of equality. There is also the deep distrust of forming partnerships with white working-class people who have exhibited tendencies to perpetuate harmful racist ideas and practices. Both of these positions are exemplified in a passage from W. E. B. Du Bois's autobiography:

> I was born in a world which was not simply fundamentally capitalistic, but had no conception of any system except one in which capital was privately owned. What I wanted was the same economic opportunities that white Americans had. Although a student of social progress, I did not know the labor development in the United States. I was bitter at lynching, but not moved by the treatment of white

miners in Colorado or Montana. I never sang the songs of Joe Hill, and the terrible strike at Lawrence, Massachusetts, did not stir me, because I knew that factory strikers like these would not let a Negro work beside them or live in the same town.

The latter issue prevents any real working-class solidarity, because as Marable puts it in *How Capitalism Underdeveloped Black America*, "For many working-class whites, the Afro-American is less a person and more a *symbolic index* between themselves and the abyss of absolute poverty." Though it amounts to little more than a psychological trick: so long as the racial caste system remains in place, poor and working-class whites will never be at the bottom.

This has not inhibited the development of black leftists with a socialist politics, but the skepticism of working alongside a white working class that has not developed an anti-racist politics has often been a barrier to coalition building with white leftists who have romanticized a multiracial working class uprising without wanting to address this very issue. Although their material interests, in the strictest sense, are closely aligned, there remain points of conflict rooted in the organizing principles of white supremacy that have a tendency to be written off as merely distractions, when they are crucial to understanding the distrust and forming a politics that poses a true threat to all forms of hierarchy, race included.

It was largely a theoretical debate up until 2016. The presidential run of Bernie Sanders, a self-avowed democratic socialist, for the Democratic nomination surprised the professional pundit class and even long-time Sanders supporters with how serious of a challenge it posed to Hillary Clinton. Sanders was aided by the factors that traditionally open the pathway for radical political transformation: economic devastation and grassroots movements. The financial crisis of 2008 wrecked the global economy in such a profound way that the ghosts of the Soviet Union could no longer serve as a deterrent to questioning the viability of capitalism. This opened the gate for the Occupy movement, which was nebulous as far as movements go, but gave a generation suffering under massive debt and bleak prospects the language to analyze and antagonize the elites who had profited off the misery of billions.

Sanders had spent the entirety of his political career hammering home a message of economic justice, and in 2016 it deeply resonated with a resurgent

American left seeking to reverse the unabashed reverence thrown toward the wealthy. He was not, as it were, calling for seizing the means of production, but the success of his campaign meant that ideas such as universal health care, free college, student debt cancellation, and (to a lesser but still important degree) job guarantees and universal basic income were discussed and weighed by non-leftist media, even if they were ultimately dismissed. He tapped into the growing sense among younger Americans that there is no individualist framework that will produce economic justice. Individual safety and prosperity at the expense of solidarity can only ever replicate capitalist hierarchies and the violent means of imposing them. If you view your emancipation as separate from mine, we will forever be locked in unwinnable competition.

But as the leftmost candidacy, and one with unforeseen excitement surrounding it, Sanders's campaign bore the burden of representation for the splintered leftist factions that had emerged as a result of various forms of political unrest. Young people, disaffected and yearning for new political realities, hoped to find expression for their causes of immigration reform, ending police violence and mass incarceration, and reproductive rights in the Sanders campaign.

Sanders, for his part, broadly shared their concern for these issues, though at times he clumsily articulated his support. His 2016 run was never meant to be a campaign to actually become president—early on he seemed to be running to place more focus on the causes he had championed throughout his career, which had to do with reining in the robber barons of Wall Street, taxing the wealthy, getting money out of our political system, and paying for programs aimed at the universal welfare. His message resonated with the movement building that had preceded his presidential run and charged up a generation of voters who had grown frustrated with the lack of bold ideas proffered by the Democratic establishment during the Obama years. But Sanders had such a singular focus on economic issues that it brought its own frustrations to the multiracial, multigender coalition forming around him. When confronted on this, he would tend to pivot back to his long-standing messaging, while some of his more obstinate supporters dismissed the specific racialized or gendered concerns of anyone questioning Sanders's broader economic platform as engaging in a divisive form of identity politics.

That term, *identity politics*, has been bandied about in ways that do not reflect its origins, such as it often goes with concepts that start at the margins and later penetrate the mainstream. In the mid-1970s, a group of black feminist scholars and activists began meeting in Boston to form an organization that would address the political concerns of black women, which they felt had been ignored by the larger feminist movement. The group included renowned poet Audre Lorde, celebrated scholar and activist Barbara Smith, and future First Lady of New York City Chirlane McCray, among others. They called themselves the Combahee River Collective, taking their name from the South Carolina site where the abolitionist Harriet Tubman led a military campaign that freed more than 750 enslaved people in 1863.

In 1977, the group issued "A Black Feminist Statement," the culmination of their work to clarify their politics, "while at the same time doing political work within our own group and in coalition with other progressive organizations and movements." They made clear that they were "actively committed to struggling against racial, sexual, heterosexual, and class oppression" and that they saw black feminism as "the logical political movement to combat the manifold and simultaneous oppressions that all women of color face." Having found that other groups—including the civil rights, Black Power, and feminist movements—were lacking in their approach to ending the oppression of black women and women of color, the collective wrote: "We realize that the only people who care enough about us to work consistently for our liberation is us. . . . This focusing on our own oppression is embodied in the concept of identity politics. We believe that the most profound and potentially the most radical politics come directly out of our own identity, as opposed to working to end somebody else's oppression."

The worst misreading of Combahee's theorizing has been to suggest that identity politics means being hostile and unsympathetic toward any issue that does not directly relate back to one's own identity, though that charge is most often lobbed at those who are nonwhite, non-cis, non-hetero, and non-male. Any political framework emanating from outside the established norm is rarely taken seriously, and most often is outright chastised for being a distraction from larger, loftier, unifying goals.

But identity politics, as laid out by the women of Combahee, is not the selfish politics it has been caricatured to be. It is a result of their belief, as they write later in the statement, that "if Black women were free, it would mean that everyone else would have to be free since our freedom would necessitate the destruction of all the systems of oppression." The original intent of identity politics was articulating black women's struggle at the nexus of race, gender, sexual, and class oppressions, and then forming strategies for dismantling each of these, both in black feminist spaces and in coalition with other groups. Questions of identity are inherently questions of power. The inclusion of black women, as the historian Keeanga-Yamahtta Taylor puts it in *Monthly Review*, "on their own terms is not a concession to 'political correctness' . . . it is necessary to validate the particular experiences of Black women in our society while also measuring exactly the levels of oppression, inequality, and exploitation experienced in African American communities."

This may appear to run counter to a socialist politics that emphasizes the benefits of the universal, but in reality it is a corrective to a level of misplaced faith that the universal has the capacity to rescue us all. The "we" has historically been exclusionary, even in moments of genuine progress. To ensure this is not our future, the universal has to be explicitly defined, or else it cannot be defended. It will, otherwise, replicate the exact lines of power and hierarchy from which we seek to escape.

Consider the New York City of the 1950s and '60s that saw a huge migration of black southerners and Puerto Ricans, which meant an expansion of the city's public school rolls. Soon enough, the neighborhood schools these children attended became grossly overcrowded. There was no legal segregation in place in New York City, but rather than send these children to schools where predominantly white children were, it was decided that the black and Puerto Rican children in the overcrowded schools would attend school on half-day shifts. And, as historian Jeanne Theoharis writes in *A More Beautiful and Terrible History*, "Black and Puerto Rican teachers were hired at much lower rates than were white teachers" in large part because the "hiring process included an oral, in-person test designed to weed out people with 'foreign' or 'Southern' accents." This, where an ostensibly universal public school system had no legal mandate for discrimination.

So it should come as no surprise that there are people who are not completely trusting of any organizing theory that claims universal aims without having accounted for the varied and interlocking systems of oppression that contribute to material and psychic degradation. An incomplete theory is not an invalid theory; socialism's antidote to capitalist exploitation is critical for any program of defeating white supremacist heteropatriarchy. But it would be impossible to transition to a multiracial, multigender democratic socialism from a white supremacist heteropatriarchal capitalism without being intentional about ending each aspect.

Otherwise, we remain subject to them even as we critique some of the most destructive practices these systems have developed. When I moved to New York City in 2013, the city was on the verge of electing a new mayor to replace Michael Bloomberg after his unprecedented third term. The election had largely become a referendum on the policing tactic that had come to be known as "stop-and-frisk," though these interactions were often more violent and damaging than the moniker lets on. In what was meant to be a preemptive crime-prevention measure (an outgrowth of the broken windows theory of policing), police stopped any individual they deemed suspicious, questioned them on the street, frisked their person in search of contraband (with or without the cooperation of the "suspect"), and at their discretion issued court summonses that carried fines for failing to appear. This practice, of course, disproportionately targeted black and Latinx communities. It was both discriminatory and ineffective in its stated goals, as most stops yielded no illegal weapons, but it did achieve the unstated goal of putting black and Latinx New Yorkers on high alert; stop-and-frisk sent the message that black and brown people are subjects to be surveilled and violated to provide white people with a sense of safety.

Stop-and-frisk was deemed unconstitutional in *Floyd v. City of New York* shortly before the mayoral election, but taking a stand against the practice—one rooted in his personal story of a white father concerned for the safety of his black children—helped propel Bill de Blasio, then serving as New York City's public advocate, to victory. De Blasio had been an activist, a campaign manager, and a city councilmember before being chosen as public advocate, and he was also married to the aforementioned Chirlane McCray, whose black feminist activism was well documented and included her 1979 essay in *Essence* titled "I Am a Lesbian." After more than a decade of Bloomberg's implementation of a police state, relief seemed on the horizon in the form of genuine progressives taking the mantle of power.

Except that one of de Blasio's first acts as mayor was to hire as police commissioner Bill Bratton, the chief architect of broken windows policing, who had previously served as NYPD commissioner under Rudy

Giuliani, before moving to the West Coast and refining the overreaching, violent techniques of the already notorious LAPD.

It was a disappointing move by the new, supposedly progressive, mayor, to say the least, one that angered the communities that helped to elect him. But de Blasio assured everyone it would be the right move, that Bratton's knowledge and experience was what the city needed in order to end the practice of stop-and-frisk while also continuing to drive down crime rates.

Sure enough, the number of reported instances of stop-and-frisk went down, though some argue the practice has continued more informally. But what also happened is that the NYPD shifted its focus. Within the first few months of de Blasio/Bratton's tenure, arrests for panhandling went up, while arrests for other low-level infractions like open containers saw an increase, and the dancers on the subway, colloquially referred to as the "Showtime!" kids, were suddenly being arrested and charged with reckless endangerment.

The New York City subway is a haven for hustlers, because where else are you guaranteed such an audience? New Yorkers, with their constant bombardment of stimuli, have fine-tuned their ability to ignore, but on the subway they are still for long enough to maybe turn their head in your direction. So the mariachi bands and the kids with the "found" boxes of candy and folks hawking homemade wares all make their way through the cars in search of a few kind faces with a few extra dollars. My personal favorite is the "Subtations," a group of slightly past middle-aged black men who harmonize voices that time and some substances have clearly taken their toll on, yet they still evoke the good feelings of the Motown classics they sing together.

The "Showtime!" kids are a major part of this ecosystem, announcing their arrival with a collective shout of "Showtime!" while clearing out space for their routine, which at their most entertaining typically involves aerial tricks using the poles that only someone with both the athleticism and impulsiveness of these young people should ever try. But I've never seen anyone harmed during these dances—some people are annoyed by the loud music, or wish they didn't have to give up their spot by the train's doors in order to make way for the show, but it is incredibly rare, to the point of being a negligible statistic, to see anyone catch a stray arm or leg to their person.

That the NYPD began arresting these kids, invariably young black and brown kids, for their dances, just as it was ending the era of stop-and-frisk, speaks to the ways a system committed to the ideology of oppression transforms only its techniques of enforcement. Where stop-and-frisk allowed officers carte blanche discretion in determining who was suspicious, this new focus simply provided a new rationale for reaching the same conclusions: harass and arrest black, brown, and poor people. And they could do so under the guise of public safety.

But who was Eric Garner harming when Daniel Pantaleo choked him to death? Garner had been accused of selling loose cigarettes and, fed up with the constant harassment he faced at the hands of police, he told them he was no longer putting up with it. His death was captured on film.

And now, as I write this, the police are arresting fare beaters on our barely functional subway system. All this has taken place under Mayor de Blasio because the mandates of progressive policing are exactly the same as those of authoritarian policing, which is to say that policing is policing no matter the adjective you put in front of it.

We are asked to hold the people in uniform in high regard because they keep us safe, but never asked whether or not we actually feel safe or what we would need in order to feel safe. "Police are not public, nor good," writes movement lawyer Derecka Purnell in *Boston Review*, if we genuinely consider the definition of "public" as encompassing all of us, which history shows we do not. The police are the enemies of black people, Latinx people, trans people, and poor people. Is it our duty to revere them, even as their presence conflicts with our freedom? After Ferguson? After Baltimore?

And isn't it funny how language works? How I can write "Ferguson" or "Baltimore" or "Trayvon" and collapse time, space, and action into a single word, with you, the reader, sure that you know exactly what I mean? There is so much violence we do with and to language, such a flattening of worlds that requires our expanded understanding.

Consider that up until this point I have used the term "American" to mean a citizen of the United States, as most of us do, when the name applies to a whole hemisphere. But US hegemony, and narcissism, is such that "American" and "America" are synonymous with our country, and we don't even realize that other Americans laugh at us for claiming ownership of that identity. Being an empire means we don't actually have to care.

Still, it does damage to the ways in which we perceive the world. "Language organizes time, space, and matter in such a way that they become recognizable to human consciousness," the theorist Franco Berardi writes in *Breathing*, and yet we are so careless with it. Which is why I make it a point, when asked, "What would you have us do with the police?" To say unequivocally, "Abolish them," because it is what I mean. I seek a world without police. When I explain that in order to achieve such a world it would require us to enact a number of redistributive policies and educational programs aimed at providing for everyone's basic needs and reducing violence, both interpersonal and state-sanctioned, that would make policing obsolete, I'm asked why I don't lead with that rather than the potentially alienating "abolish police." And my answer is that I believe in stating, in clear language, what you want because otherwise you are beholden to the current state of consciousness and accepted wisdom. I want a world in which the police do not exist, and there is no clearer way to say it.

In the past, I have been accused of hating the police. And I do. Such an admission may be taken to mean that I hate each police officer as an individual whom I have judged unfairly on the basis of their occupation.

But I hate the police the same as I hate any institution that exists as an obstruction to justice. It's important here to define justice, as the US legal system has perverted our sense of what constitutes it. It cannot be punishment or retribution for harm caused. Justice is not revenge. Rather, justice is a proactive commitment to providing each person with the material and social conditions in which they can both survive and thrive as a healthy and self-actualized human being. This is not an easy thing to establish, as it requires all of us buying into the idea that we must take responsibility for one another. But it is the only form of a just world.

The police have never been—historically, presently, in statement of purpose, nor in action—and I believe will never be capable of fostering such conditions. And so I hate them because I have grown past impatient with injustice. I am incensed by the delusion, so prevalent among the country's supposedly serious thinkers, that tinkering around the edges of an inherently oppressive institution will lead to freedom.

The police are needed only insofar as there is a need to police the borders of the American—pardon me, US—identity, meaning that they are needed to determine who is worthy of life, liberty, and happiness. The same number of police deployed to arrest a solitary drug dealer in my neighborhood are also sent to protect Confederate statues from being torn down; the use of police teaches us who and what is valued.

Police are sent to the southern border to put children in cages so that white people can be less fearful of one day being outnumbered. They are not called police because policing is reserved for people who are nominally citizens, but they function just as police do: they stop, question, frisk, arrest, detain, harass, intimidate, and enforce laws meant to keep undesirable people in their place. It's a great paradox of empire—a virtually borderless country that fiercely enforces its artificial borders. America is attempting to regulate who belongs where on a planet it is making nearly uninhabitable.

Of course, that reality makes these decisions even more dire. We are facing an end. We are up against climate disaster. Cities will disappear, infrastructure will be destroyed, huge populations will be displaced. The droughts in Central America are already pushing migrants to seek shelter and asylum here, while they are called gang members and terrorists. The rains from Hurricane Maria sent Puerto Ricans to south Florida and forced an uncomfortable conversation to take place among the Americans who have long ignored the island's existence.

The angry refrain after it was clear the Trump administration would leave people to die was that Puerto Ricans are Americans, too, though the official status of the island is "foreign in a domestic sense," an oxymoron more neatly and accurately captured by a single word: colony. Graffiti in Old San Juan states it plainly: "Welcome to the Oldest Colony." I walked those streets a month before Maria hit. It's not that everyone on the island yearns for independence—it's a truly contentious topic, with passion on all sides— but there has been enough discontent with more than a century of languishing as property of the United States, and having recently had their local government's powers essentially stripped away, that the anger was being reflected all over. "Fuck Gentrification, Gringo Go Home," another hastily written piece read. "Esta 'Democracia' No La Entendemos," read another, with a drawing of Lady Justice underneath, only one of her eyes covered. It means "We Do Not Understand This 'Democracy.'" There isn't much to understand. Democratic nations do not have colonies. This is empire.

And the empire watched as its subjects drowned, as thousands died, and asked why they didn't do more to save themselves, as if they had built this hell for themselves.

Would they be better off as citizens? Perhaps the token representation such a designation would afford them within the federal government may have provided more relief. Or they could have found the same indifference to their rising waters that residents of Flint have found to their poisoned waters. Being American does not make you American—that is, being American is not a promise you will receive everything promised to Americans.

Indifference, here, feels like a word that lacks the necessary heft to convey the magnitude of this atrocity. The people of Flint had their water, the most meaningful of all resources for human survival, poisoned through thoroughly undemocratic deals meant only to bolster the profits of a private corporation and its stakeholders. The health effects are only beginning to be known to us. But they are largely poor, mostly black, and so their safety is of little concern. No one will call the police on their behalf.

If, however, they sat on the floor of city hall, demanding their pipes be updated, their water be clean again, police would appear and they would arrest them for causing a disturbance. If they resisted too much, or maybe got too mouthy for an officer's liking, they could be sure they would be arrested, if not also struck before being arrested. If the effort to get them out wasn't working fast enough, they would almost certainly be teargassed.

People who have everything stolen from them are scolded for not doing more to prevent the theft, but when they assert themselves in a manner that is a direct challenge to power, they are met with violence. It happened at Standing Rock. They meant to prevent their water from being poisoned, not unlike it had been in Flint. The United States was breaking yet another treaty with the indigenous people, rerouting an oil pipeline through their land because the original route was protested by people who feared it would contaminate their water supply, as an oil pipeline is prone to do. And the US government abided their concerns, because when you are white and well-off, you are an American with all the attendant privileges. If you are Native, meaning you are descendant of those who survived the initial genocide that made this land Anglo property, you are not American; you never have been, and likely you have never wanted to be. But you have wanted your sovereignty respected, that which was promised to you by the progeny of the original oppressors. But the more they wanted, the more they took. And at Standing Rock they wanted their pipeline, so they would ignore another treaty, take more land, poison the water of the non-Americans. The protesters did not call themselves protesters; they said they were water protectors.

That a person must take on such a role is an indicator that there is no justice here. That they were the enemy makes it clear, as climate disaster looms, the pimps have not ceased their pursuit of profits at the expense of the rest of us. So the police were sent in to make certain the water protectors would not win. When they wouldn't move, they turned water cannons on them. That which gives life was turned into a weapon to protect capital.

I thought, then, of the old civil rights—era footage of the police turning water hoses on children, strong and painful streams meant to extinguish fires. I recall being taught about those children's bravery in the face of hatred. I don't remember any condemnation of the people on the other side, holding the hose, spraying the small, unarmed children called upon to be brave to change a society resistant to justice for all. I remember being told a story of heroes with no villains.

As a New York State assemblyperson at the tail end of what we call the civil rights movement, Shirley Chisholm introduced legislation that would have mandated police officers complete courses in civil rights, civil liberties, "minority problems, and race relations" before they could serve. It obviously did not pass, but had it done so it would have, in my estimation, ended policing altogether. No person, in good conscious, having completed such a curriculum, would then be able to go about the duties of a police officer. No one could come out of such a course, if it were taught honestly and thoroughly, still believing there is such a thing as good policing. I like to think Chisholm knew this when she introduced the legislation. It's a bit of projection, but the actual vision she displayed is not less worthy of praise.

By the time the next president is inaugurated and New York City is deciding on a new mayor, there will be a statue of Shirley Chisholm standing in Prospect Park, a part of an initiative to have more statues honoring women placed throughout the city. Others will be erected for Billie Holiday, Helen Rodríguez Trías,

Elizabeth Jennings Graham, and Katherine Walker. Not too long ago, not far from where the statue of Chisholm will eventually be placed, I spotted a white woman wearing a T-shirt that read "Make Empathy Great Again." It's also not far from where I saw four or five police officers take down a homeless man's makeshift shelter. He had set it up in front of the train station, where in the summer a farmers' market sells all kinds of organic, fresh, seasonal fruits and vegetables. Pastries, too. He was bothering no one, simply surviving as best he could as the weather changed. But the police came anyway, threw his belongings on the ground, tore down the rather impressive structure, and moved the man along.

In her time as a US congressperson, Chisholm helped create the national school lunch program and expanded the food stamps program. Someday soon there will be someone sleeping in the shadow of her statue.

PART 3

ACCOUNTABILITY

"I know every bit of that, Sethe. I wasn't born yesterday and I never mistreated a woman in my life."

"That makes one in the world," Sethe answered.
—Toni Morrison, *Beloved*

What is, so to speak, the object of abolition? Not so much the abolition of prisons but the abolition of a society that could have prisons, that could have slavery, that could have the wage, and therefore not abolition as the elimination of anything but abolition as the founding of a new society.
—Fred Moten and Stefano Harvey, *The Undercommons*

Before I moved to New York, my understanding of the city was shaped, like that of so many others, by the culture I consumed. It was a place to be survived. As a child, I knew it as the place where the hardest of the hardcore came up hearing gunshots every night, and Biggie declared that escape was only possible through crack sales or basketball skills. In my early twenties, it became the place where nebbish Woody Allen types went to contemplate their own mortality with other people who had read Camus.

When I first visited in 2009, it was neither of these things, but also both of them, and yet something else entirely. The city cannot be reduced because it attracts all kinds. I've grown fond of saying that no matter your particular brand of crazy, New York has people to match it, and they'll help you feel less alone. And it's true, there are communities here, despite its reputation to outsiders as a hostile place. Admittedly, I still don't look up at any tall buildings, out of fear that I'll be seen as a tourist, which is another word for easy mark, and be pickpocketed while staring in wonderment. It's unlikely, but the threat of my imagined New York looms.

What I have actually found here is not nearly as dramatic as what I had conjured. There are more eccentrics, but there is more of everything here. It is a city of surplus, unequally distributed. It's in this abundance that artists find their material, though the abundant resources may differ. Woody Allen had an abundance of white intellectuals in his world, while Biggie had an abundance of guns and drugs, and both had, in their own ways, an abundance of despair.

Bill Cosby created a 1980s Brooklyn landscape out of abundance, though his chosen resource was more fantastical. I didn't grow up on *The Cosby Show*; I was born in 1986, when the show had already been a hit for two years, and by the time I was at the age where I might watch television that wasn't primarily cartoons, the show was no longer in production. I know it best through reruns in syndication. But I grew up in the world that *The Cosby Show* helped to shape. Cosby had a vision for a television show that depicted a black middle-class family that wasn't preoccupied with its blackness and existed in a world that cast a similar attitude toward it. It is the stuff of pure fantasy, a very appealing fantasy whether you are a black viewer or a white one. For black viewers, it was a chance, for thirty minutes, to feel less encumbered by the dangers of American racism to the black body and psyche. The Huxtables had hold of the American Dream, and it could feel as though they were keeping space for the rest of us to come grab hold of it too.

Except that was all fanciful daydreaming. The Huxtables were not real. Cliff Huxtable was an unrecognizable character by design. Not that there had never been well-off black people before—of course there had been. But Cliff Huxtable seemed to be a black man born in 1940s America with no resentment, no disappointment, no scars from racism, married to a black woman who held a similar outlook, raising black children in 1980s Brooklyn who also never came up against any obstacles that were not products of their own comical ineptitude. They never rode the subway, they never heard any gunshots, they never had any block parties, they never hung out on the stoop or the rooftop, they never had any violent encounters with police, they never passed by drug dealers, they never worried about anything beyond a humorous lecture from their father and a stern look from their mother. They are not a part of any world that has ever actually existed.

For white viewers, there was absolution. You thought he was funny, maybe you even found her attractive, and the children relatable, so here was proof, definitively, that you had room for acceptance of black people after all. It had nothing to do with race—they rarely even mentioned it, so you never thought about it. For thirty minutes, a color-blind reality, wherein white people had no responsibility for black success or failure, was possible.

This was Cosby's goal. It was very much his show. It carries his name, though no character in this imagined world is similarly named Cosby. Cliff and Bill are presumed to be one and the same, because Bill could fulfill his fantasy through Cliff. He asked that we believe there was no difference between the creator and his creation. And we did. So much so that Cosby, the real man, was deemed "America's Dad" and the nation turned to him for parenting advice because Cliff, the fictional character, seemed to have figured it out so well. So much so that it seemed impossible to imagine Bill committing heinous acts of violence on so many women, across so many years.

There are 60 women, in 19 different cities, who have accused Cosby of sexual assault or harassment, and many of them also allege that he drugged them.

He was only convicted of assaulting one woman. Her name is Andrea Constand. The assaults he is accused of date back to the mid-1960s, and don't end until the late 2000s. The first time I remember them being reported was in 2004, not long after he delivered his infamous "pound cake" speech, in which he chastised poor black Americans for not living up to their end of the bargain—for failing to take advantage of the opportunities opened up to them by virtue of the civil rights movement and doing more to move themselves out of poverty. But those accusations came and went, and Bill Cosby's life moved along. Until it didn't.

Bill Cosby will, in all likelihood, die in prison. He was eighty years old when he was convicted on three counts of "aggravated indecent assault," and eighty-one when he was sentenced to three to ten years in a state prison. The only way that he will not die in prison is if he, by dent of a miracle, is able to survive despite his already poor health, and is released after serving the minimum of his sentence. It is hard to imagine this outcome.

It is also hard to think of Bill Cosby in prison and not think of Cliff Huxtable in prison. Which is what Bill Cosby has wanted us to think. In part, it's how he was able to get away with assaulting so many women for as long as he did. But this was all Bill. It was Bill, not Cliff, who gained these women's trust and, when they were unaware of his movements, slipped pills into their drinks. It was Bill who watched as these women got woozy, unable to keep consciousness. And then it was Bill who undressed them, who violated them, who acted as if nothing happened, or as if they had been fully present with him and wanted it the entire time.

Cliff Huxtable was not there in those rooms. Cliff Huxtable is an impossible fantasy created by Bill Cosby. And Bill Cosby is only a man. One who will likely die in prison.

I do not say that to downplay the violence he enacted. What he did, what he has been convicted of and what he has actually admitted to doing, is monstrous. These are deliberate and depraved acts of violence committed with no regard for the humanity and dignity of the women who were forced to experience them. Still, Bill Cosby is only a man. He is a man who learned what it is to be a man from other men, who themselves learned what it is to be a man from other men, all of whom have had something to gain from the definition of manhood being violent and depraved. What I am saying is that there are many Bill Cosbys still with us now. They will not all die in prison.

They will continue to teach other boys and men what it is to be men. They will teach girls and women what it is to be men too. They will tell them what to expect from men, and why it is necessary for men to be that way. They will rationalize and justify, excuse and deny, manipulate and lie their way toward more power, more domination, more depravity. They will look like Cliff Huxtable.

And Brett Kavanaugh. Yes, they will coach girls' basketball and sit on the Supreme Court. And Harvey Weinstein. They will be the gatekeepers of Hollywood's prestige films. And Matt Lauer. They will be the country's best-compensated journalists, determining what stories should and should not be told, as well as how to tell them. And R. Kelly. They will take advantage of a national disinterest in the protection of black girls, and have others aid them in their reign of abuse and assault. And Donald Trump. They will become president.

And you will go to church with them. You will shop for groceries alongside them. They will be your next-door neighbor, and you may borrow hardware from them. They will be in your college study group. You will match with them on dating sites. You will attend a protest with them. They will give you no reason to suspect them. You will pass them every day and never know their names.

This would seem to be an infinite hellscape, violent men lurking everywhere, undetectable. If this is the current situation, it would make sense, to any rational mind, for there to be more rape, more violence, more assault than there is now. It should be happening every minute, every second, everywhere.

It is. It is happening constantly. Not without notice, but without the notice of those who would rather not know. It is happening more than the numbers can tell us because the numbers can only tell us who has spoken up; the numbers cannot tell us how many live in fear that their voice will be the thing to kill them. They do not tell us how many cannot speak.

So it has happened, is happening, and will continue to happen, should this world go unchanged. And not only will it continue to happen, the men who are not actually Bill Cosby—those who are not public figures whose entire persona is a contrived antithesis to their brutal reality, who have not left a trail of victims spanning decades—but are nonetheless guilty of inflicting scars, will never know what it is to be held accountable.

These men, if they are revealed, will find communities ready and willing to defend them, to castigate their victims for daring to make the accusation in the first place. They will be reassured that they have done nothing wrong, that they are guilty only of being men and there has never been anything wrong with being a man.

As my neighborhood continues to be remade for the growing number of young white people moving in, there is often construction happening that makes certain streets or sidewalks inaccessible. Of course, O. Henry's famous quip about New York City—"It'll be a great place if they ever finish it"—still holds and might suggest that the work being done in my neighborhood is not unique, that it is only part of the larger, unending project of New York City, constantly in a state of becoming. But ask the people who have lived here the longest and they will conspiratorially wonder aloud why these long-needed repairs to the roads are only taking place now.

Anyway, what all this work means is that there are always crews in hard hats outside, and with them bright orange warning signs. These signs are familiar across the country, urging CAUTION or directing cars to drive SLOW. One reads MEN AT WORK.

There is no need to update this sign to reflect more gender diversity in construction jobs—there are only men at work here. It's a strange announcement, since there are other signs that say SIDEWALK CLOSED, which feels to me a very clear message that you should not proceed. But MEN AT WORK signals something of great importance is happening here that must not be disturbed, and that there are grave consequences if they are. In all likelihood, the men will just tell you that you can't walk or drive there, that you must find an alternative route, and everyone will go about their lives. But the MEN AT WORK sign warns that it should not get to this point, as you should respect and be deferential toward these men as they go about the business of being men at work.

I don't want it to be misunderstood, as though I have some contempt for these men. They are not police. They are doing work that is actually necessary. The maintenance of the city infrastructure is important, difficult, physically exhausting, fairly dangerous work. However, I find the gendered MEN AT WORK sign curious as an expression of masculine primacy. I take issue with there needing to be some bright pronouncement of the gender of people doing the work because it is saying, in part, that it is the gender that makes the work serious and therefore worthy of the world's notice—that these MEN AT WORK should go undisturbed and unquestioned.

But these are not rich men, not titans of industry, not capitalist robber barons. They are labor, earning an honest dollar for honest work. They are not responsible for the politics of who stays and who goes, who is cared for and who is not. They, too, are the working class.

But they have been recruited to participate in the displacement of other working-class people, and since they are MEN AT WORK, it is expected that critics of such displacement will have no space to complain.

We are charged to always keep this in mind: men are doing important work, and to interrupt them is to halt the gears of a functioning society.

So the men go about their work, important or not, believing themselves the only ones capable of it. The monuments they build to their own sense of significance become markers of space where others are not allowed. They demand the world's celebration and submission. Their work becomes so integral to the ways in which we understand the world that we cannot escape their influence, even if we know what harm Woody Allen and Biggie have done.

Then the men, because they have taught themselves that the world is their possession and have forced everyone else to accept this as truth, do what anyone does when they possess something they have never truly learned to care for: they wreck it.

The people who are not men find themselves on the receiving end of this wreckage, both abused by the men and also convinced they are beholden to them. It is, they have been told, the men's genius, strength, labor, intuition, and guile that created the world that makes life possible, and the people who are not men should be grateful. They should be more than willing to pay the price for their existence here, even when the cost is their body, their dignity, their basic claim to humanity.

What men have underestimated, and perhaps always will—though maybe it is not an underestimation so much as it is a wild delusion that those who are not men actually like the world order men have created—is the countervailing power that pushes against manhood. Men have become so enraptured by their own definition of power, one steeped in the ideology of domination, coercion, manipulation, violence, and thievery (all undemocratic forms of rule), that they fail to take note of the forms of power building around them based on cooperation, compassion, healing, and a shared interest in each other's survival. When men meet this kind of power, they are stunned, largely because they have never been tasked with conceiving of a world in which their own dominance was not taken as a given. They are not prepared to be taken down by what they have rendered weak.

And so Harvey Weinstein fled the country because he never imagined that his victims would speak, let alone speak together. And the more abused people who spoke up, the more men who fell, because they had never anticipated the power that could come from beneath them. The world they built had not been structured that way.

Weinstein is headed off to prison. R. Kelly may be too. Some of the men are falling, and as satisfying as that may be, the punishment they face also feels insufficient to mitigate the level of harm that they caused. Bill Cosby will probably die in prison, but do we claim this as justice? It hardly even qualifies as accountability. Prison is a form of punishment that is an evasion of both these principles. Prison, as Angela Davis put it in *Are Prisons Obsolete?*, "relieves us of the responsibility of seriously engaging with the problems of our society." Aside from the bloodlust that sits inside the notion that the imprisoned get what they deserve, what is appealing about prison is that it disappears the individuals who have been designated as the problem. The existence of prison allows those of us outside of its walls to avoid a confrontation with deeper systemic issues by neatly defining who is a good or bad actor. Such a binary simplifies our decision-making—the bad must be separated from the good or else the good risk putting themselves in harm's way.

But even if we take as true that each individual human action can be issued an absolute moral judgment of good or bad (which I don't believe we can, but for a moment we will assume this position), determining whether a person, who will inevitably do both good and bad things, is either wholly good or wholly bad is an impossible task. There is no infallible formula for weighing each action against the other, no way to keep score for each of us. To rely on the law to sort us is to assign a moral clarity to the laws that is unachievable by the people who conceive of them. The law is incapable of making such determinations, as the law is not an arbiter of what is moral. Legal versus illegal is a distinction that allows the powerful the imprimatur of moral authority, but what becomes illegal is not always that which is most harmful to the societal fabric, but rather that which the powerful have deemed inconvenient to their maintenance of power. It is not illegal to gather without a permit because it is immoral; it is illegal because it is a showing of force that has disruptive potential. Illicit drugs are not categorized as such because they present a grave danger to our health, but because the illegality provides the pretense for the greater surveillance and police state (and as the benefits of legalizing drugs become clear, the powerful will change their opinion alongside the new chase for profit). The law, therefore, cannot measure the goodness of a person who is subjected to it.

On the occasion of his own sentencing on the charge of sedition in 1918, socialist organizer Eugene V. Debs said: "While there is a lower class, I am in it; while there is a criminal element, I am of it; while there is a soul in prison, I am not free." It is a romantic idea to align oneself with the outlaws who flaunt their disobedience to societal rules, and even righteous to identify with those who have been wrongly convicted by an unjust system. These are the sympathetic figures who expose the rot at the heart of these criminal institutions. But the prisons do not only house the righteous and wronged. What would it mean to also identify with the rapist—a person guilty of a truly heinous act—not as a rapist, but as another human?

I ask about the rapist because they are usually the first example used to make the case for the necessity of prison. Serial killers are a close second. But there exists little of the cultural curiosity with regard to rapists as there is serial killers, who are the subjects of TV shows, movies, books, fan clubs, et cetera. This does not engender sympathy for convicted rapists but does make them, for some, less bothersome as a social problem. Rhetorically, at least. For all the posturing about rape as reprehensible and unacceptable, the number of those convicted of rape comes nowhere close to the number of rapes committed, while those who are accused are given the benefit of the doubt no matter the evidence.

Still, rhetorically, rape is recognized as one of the few human actions that can be assessed sans any moral ambiguity—it is wrong. Rape serves no other function aside from the complete dehumanization of another person and the consolidation of violent hierarchies.

A logical conclusion to draw of a person who commits rape, then, would be that they are unambiguously bad. It is a conclusion that is difficult to argue against, but only if you continue to find the binary useful.

Identifying the rapist as bad will help you send them away, but it will not help to prevent the rape.

We have essentially conceded that rape, or at the very least the potential of rape, is a part of our societal makeup. Those most likely to be victims are taught how to avoid it (learn self-defense, carry mace, don't walk alone at night, don't wear revealing clothing, don't drink too much, don't leave your drink unattended, don't go home with strangers, and on and on and on), while those most likely to be perpetrators are given no instruction in not becoming rapists. It is assumed that only the monsters among them will ever do such a profoundly monstrous thing.

On Wednesdays at noon, I have therapy in a neighborhood where the few people who look like me are typically pushing strollers filled with children who do not look like them. I don't wish there were more of us there, living alongside people who barely acknowledge our existence, so much as I wish these caregivers' work was appropriately valued. The point here, though, is that people who look like me in that neighborhood stand out. So when, one afternoon after therapy, I was approached at the train station by a young black woman with a curly, sandy blonde afro who waved one hand at me, and held a clipboard in her other, trying to get me to stop, I was already taken aback by her mere presence.

"Hello, you look like you care about women," she said, and I didn't know how to respond. I knew this line was rehearsed, intended to be a deliberate manipulation of a person's desire to be seen as good. I was also left to wonder what that would actually mean, if it were possible to look as if you care about women. What sort of fashion choices might reveal that you care? Or would it be something about the eyes and mouth?

I would be all too happy to know that I look like such a person, but I also know that if it is possible to construct this image, then it is replicable by anyone, whether they care about women or not. This is precisely what Bill Cosby did.

I am not Bill Cosby, but such an admission does more work to elide responsibility than it does to comfort those who fear becoming victims. They remain on guard because there is no formula for knowing who cares (or what that person's particular definition of "care" consists of) and because the monster could be any one of us—men—who have been socialized into believing there is the promise of power in our violence. Any one of us who have learned that we are entitled to the bodies of others is capable of putting those bodies in danger.

What then would it mean to understand such violence, and those who are responsible for it, as utterly and disturbingly human? Not in such a way that makes us feel compassion but that gets us to accept that if it is human behavior, it means that we bear some responsibility for having created the conditions for it to blossom. It is also, then, behavior we have the ability to prevent by creating new conditions under which it is no longer feasible.

Such a shift would require an admission that we created such conditions, that the ignoble pursuit of status within a gendered hierarchy leaves all tactics of domination available to the in-group of power. We would be responsible for saying to one another that men teach other men to be destructive.

And then we would have to look at those men we fear who sit behind bars (as well as those who have so far escaped the system) and, without absolving them, recognize we have failed them too. Such reflection, ideally, should lead us toward an interrogation of how we reinforce the predatory and violent behavior of other men for fear that any consequences for that behavior would be a direct challenge to the power we have been able to wield for so long.

Except we are institutionally addicted to the binary, because the neat lines of morality it provides allow us to evade the call for societal reformation if we already imagine ourselves to be good. With such narrow focus on the self and a sense of personal responsibility that extends barely past a duty to politeness, if you present as good you are not a danger. You do not require further inquiry.

You can get away with behavior that would be condemned were you perceived as bad. You can call a woman a bitch, so long as you back it up with reasoning for why you would do something so out of character. You can be deceptive toward romantic and sexual partners under the guise of protecting their feelings. You can say that you admire natural beauty, when what you mean is you admire beauty that conforms to long-standing notions of femininity that you perceive as effortless. You can repress your own uncomfortable feelings until they lead you to act out in ways that are at first self-destructive but have ramifications for those closest to you as well, because you have made decisions about what everyone else is capable of handling. You can claim you listen to and support women but only do so when you think of them as sexually available, rescind that support when they prove not to be, and never think twice about it. You can talk over women to tell them about how you know you shouldn't talk over women. You can keep saying "I'm still learning" even when the lesson has been taught to you a dozen times over. You can pepper your speech with all the correct terminology and still fail to properly address trans and gender nonconforming people. You can separate the art from the artist and not consider their victims when you press play.

You can do a whole host of bad things when you have convinced the rest of the world you are good.

Sometimes, reader, I write "you" when I'm too afraid to admit my own failures. Sometimes I'm a coward. I am a coward more often than not.

My life is structured around my own cowardice. I live where I do in part because I have a fairly reliable (as far as the MTA goes) train nearby that is able to connect me to most other trains I might need to get around Brooklyn. You aren't meant to get around Brooklyn by train—they all lead into Manhattan, rather than making it possible to travel from neighborhood to neighborhood intra-borough. The architects of the subway system didn't envision a world where Brooklyn was its own destination.

I have it good compared to other friends of mine, or even my former self who lived in Bushwick and would have to travel an hour by train if I wanted to get to Crown Heights, a mere three miles away. Even in a car that trip takes about twenty minutes; New York warps your sense of time and space.

It's a bit easier for me now, as I have access to a shuttle train that gets me into Crown Heights in much less time than it would have taken years ago. The shuttle only has four stops that connect Flatbush, Crown Heights, and Bedstuy. One afternoon I was getting on the shuttle to meet a friend in Bedstuy. As I boarded, a young man approached me with a piece of paper, and I never found out what was on it because as soon as he made a move toward me I waved him off. He did nothing wrong, but I've learned to be more selfish with my time since I've lived here; there are so many people who make demands on it. He moved on, approaching others on the train, exceedingly polite in speech, no one interested in what was on his paper, what he was trying to get them to listen to or sign onto. A young woman closer to his age than I am got on the train, and he approached her. She was trying to find a seat. "Excuse me, sir," she said to him, wanting him to move so she could sit down.

"Miss, miss, miss," he responded, still looking for someone to listen to him, to find out what was on his piece of paper. She waved him off like all the others. But he persisted.

"Get out of my face," she said to him. He hadn't only persisted in trying to get her attention, he refused to move so she could take her seat. He was less polite now.

"Suck my dick, light-skinned bitch," he told her. "Suck my dick," she spat back at him. "I'll spit on you, ho," he said to her as he left the train. She took her seat and looked unbothered.

I watched the interaction unfold and hoped it wouldn't escalate past the insults. I didn't intervene. I didn't take that young man to task for his behavior or his language or anything. I sat hoping that this was the extent of the violence. I don't know what I would have done if it hadn't been.

The young woman appeared unshaken by the interaction; she proceeded to do her makeup with steady hands and continue the conversation she was having on her phone. She exuded the classic New York bravado I had heard so much about before I moved here and witnessed it for myself.

I don't know how long she had to practice and perfect that bravado. I don't know what toll it has taken on her. I know that she shouldn't have had to.

But in order for that to be true, she would need a different world to live in, where men who imagine themselves good, with seemingly perfect manners, do not snap and shift from "Miss, miss, miss" to "I'll spit on you, ho" in the span of seconds. And in the event that one does, other men who imagine themselves to be good do not sit still and hope for a return to stasis because of their own discomfort.

I should have written that in the first person. But I am often a coward. Perhaps you are too. We are not cowards because we fear violence; our lives have already been defined by so much of it. What we fear is a world in which we won't recognize ourselves. It is not change we fear, but loss. We fear losing the identity that has allowed us to survive. Manhood becomes a means of protection in a world that determines who lives and who dies based on your perceived value. Being a man signals your value to the world. Upholding the values of manhood requires active participation in diminishing the humanity of those who are not men.

It has never been the case that this *must* be what manhood is defined by, but men have shown ourselves unwilling to consider any alternatives. The perverse glee that comes with wielding coercive power against others has led men to their worst impulses, while failing to see that such power not only harms those who are subjected to its violence but also the perpetrators themselves. Men are not healthy, whole, loving, or compassionate. We are none of these things toward others and even less so toward ourselves.

In our cowardice, we choose not to acknowledge this self-harm under the mistaken idea that we will find solace through the repetition of masculine violences. But not one of us is capable of countenancing such a performance without breaking our minds and bodies. "I realized," writes the essayist Gerald Early in the *Kenyon Review*, "with a certain formidable, bristling force, how precarious manhood of any sort is in this world: what a strangely perishing thing it is."

It is such a fragile construct that it requires constant reinforcement. The boundaries of manhood are maintained in various ways, some seemingly innocuous and others more appallingly violent. And I don't believe it is any accident that in recent years, as gender constructs come under more scrutiny and traditional masculinity in particular has been met with condemnation, that the homicide rates for trans women have reached record highs. In 2017, twenty-nine trans women were killed, while in 2018 it was twenty-six. And most of these are black trans women; in June 2019, Pride Month, four black trans women were killed in the US.

"For a fact we know that black transgender women are not exposed to violence because of anything inherent in their identity," Mateo De La Torre, policy advocate at the National Center for Transgender Equality, said in a radio interview. "It is the situation in the systemic structure that we've created in our society that limits their access to employment, that limits their access to housing, that limits their access to any form of opportunity, and more often than not, funnels people into survival work." Survival work, which is largely understood as sex work or the drug trade, is illegal work, which then puts black trans women at greater risk of being targeted by law enforcement, its own form of violence, and pushes them further from the services that could be lifesaving.

But while decriminalization of sex work and the drug trade would alleviate some of the largest threats facing black trans women's survival, it would leave one major threat unaddressed: the fragility of cis men. There may not be anything inherent in black trans women's identities that exposes them to violence, as De La Torre puts it, but there is something inherent to crafting cis men's identities that makes trans women targets of their rage and subsequent violence. The very idea that there is fluidity to gender and gender expression conflicts with the rigid definitions of masculinity that cis men hold dear. Failure to accept that also means a failure to recognize trans women as women, which only leads to internalized shame for being sexually attracted to trans women, which morphs into contempt directed at trans women for "tricking" these cis men into feeling a socially unsanctioned desire. The louder the voices outside get in denigrating trans women, the greater the internal turmoil of cis men who want to be "real" men, the more contempt that is directed outward, until it finds its ultimate expression in the killing of women who wanted nothing more than to live as they are.

And still it is easy for such men to consider themselves good when the only thing they are guilty of is hurting an already devalued group of people. There is no incentive to be better when so few people come to the defense of those you have harmed.

Except that these behaviors hurt the perpetrator, as well. "If you've done fucked up shit, you know it's not that easy," legendary rapper Bun B said in an interview, not too long after he himself shot a home intruder. "You don't just shoot somebody and go home and go to sleep. It don't really work like that." It is one of our great misconceptions that the purveyors of violence do so without conscience, without repercussions to their own psyche. It is not easy to hurt another person, harder even to take a life. It is its own trauma.

And while the first priority in such a situation, it should be clear, is the victim, the lack of recognition that there is trauma on the part of the perpetrator results in the inability to have true accountability. This is an action beyond apology—accountability asks us to repair the external harm, making restitution by caring for the needs of our victims, and to undertake an internal harm reduction process, wherein we come to understand our behavioral patterns and commit to changing what has wrought harm (I owe the evolution in my thinking about accountability to Mariame Kaba, a longtime organizer and founder of Project

NIA, a grassroots organization that aims to end youth incarceration). But this work can only begin when the perpetrator is given the space to admit what they have done, transparently and honestly.

The very existence of the prison forecloses on such possibilities. With the potential of being locked away in a cage, subjected to daily humiliation, degradation, and outright torture looming over us all, the inclination is toward denial, as there are no incentives for the truth. Prison provides an out that prevents any true healing, for the perpetrators or the victims.

When *Surviving R. Kelly* director dream hampton asked the women he had preyed upon what they wanted to happen to him, "each of them pleaded with him to 'get help,' to 'just stop' hurting girls and women like them," she writes in *Time*. "[When] they considered what justice might be for an accused serial predator, they never used the words *jail* or *prison*. They wished for him a healing, that he face and own the harm he's caused." Few people actually *want* prison, most simply want what justice has been made available to them. "More than anything else, what I want is a reckoning," the essayist Lacy M. Johnson writes of her abuser and rapist in the *Paris Review*. "I don't want him dead. I want him to admit all the things he did, to my face, in public, and then to spend the rest of his life in service to other people's joy." This is not the purpose or function of prison. It fails those it is purportedly in service of protecting.

Abolition offers an alternative framework for thinking through how we care for everyone who is harmed, *and* for considering how to reduce and prevent harm from occurring. Prison is not a means of preventing violence, but for shifting it out of sight from polite society. In this way, it becomes harder to convince a society convinced of its own politeness that a confrontation with prison is necessary. Out of sight, and so on.

But this will not always be the situation. An institution does what it can to protect itself, and prison feeds on criminalization. As societal attitudes and laws change around some things, the institution will adjust to continue feeding the prison system, so long as the undergirding logic of prison goes unchecked. The privileged will be protected for only so long.

They are recognizing this now, which is why you have the Koch brothers interested in criminal legal system reform. Publicly, they say the right things, but their actual concerns are regulations that serve to criminalize actions that impede their pursuit of profits. They are on the right side of the issue for the wrong reasons, which is why it is important to strike an ideological distinction between the type of reform they seek and what an abolitionist framework asks of us. Reformers like the Koch brothers would ask that we decriminalize the abhorrent actions their corporations routinely commit so that they are never held accountable. Abolition asks that we imagine a world in which those actions are not even possible.

"Justice in abolitionist terms involves at once exposing the violence, hypocrisy, and dissembling entrenched in existing legal practices, while attempting to achieve peace, make amends, and distribute resources more equitably," legal scholar Allegra M. McLeod writes in the *Harvard Law Review*. "Justice for abolitionists is an integrated endeavor to prevent harm, intervene in harm, obtain reparations, and transform the conditions in which we live."

Or, as Angela Davis puts it: "Rather than try to imagine one single alternative to the existing system of incarceration, we might envision an array of alternatives that will require radical transformations of many aspects of our society." It is true, as skeptics will remind us, that you cannot decriminalize everything and free everyone from prison tomorrow and expect a utopia. Abolition is not such a naive proposition. It is rooted in a recognition that all our systems have been established for the purposes of oppression. While I agree with Moten and Harvey that the central project of abolition is the founding of a new society, it is not the case that it is unconcerned with the elimination of those systems that are incompatible with a just, humane, accountable, and honest society. The elimination of one of these systems requires the elimination of all, but elimination is not sufficient. Abolition asks for the building of institutions that have care—an attentiveness to people's needs and responsiveness to shifting emotions—as their core imperative and that worry less about their own existence and more about the function they serve in people's lives.

"What is denounced as 'utopian' is no longer that which has 'no place' and cannot have any place in the historical universe," the philosopher Herbert Marcuse wrote in *An Essay on Liberation*, "but rather that which is blocked from coming about by the power of the established societies." Power evades accountability by convincing us that the current order protects us all from the inevitability of chaos and constant warfare, while relying on war to maintain the establishment. What is the system afraid to lose?

A woman I love, whom I have given many reasons not to love me, said to me that true accountability is only possible when you consent to be destroyed. Initially, I asked her if I could steal that to write for you here. She said yes because where I saw theft, she saw collaboration. My old self has yet to be completely destroyed.

What person would consent to their own destruction? What nation would? It is difficult to consent to something you are convinced you won't survive.

But nothing will be solved when Bill Cosby dies in prison. It will still take an hour to get from Bushwick to Crown Heights, unless we set the intention to create a different path.

PART 4

FREEDOM

I have always lived in the myth of New York more than in its reality. It is what enabled me to live there for so long, loving the idea of something more than the thing itself.

—Ling Ma, *Severance*

Deep down, the American condition is a state of unease.

—Ralph Ellison, *Going to the Territory*

Had Shirley Chisholm won the presidential race in 1972, she would have been only the second president born in New York City and the first to come from Brooklyn. Her father was born in British Guiana (the people won their independence in 1966 and renamed their land Guyana), her mother in Barbados, where Shirley spent a good portion of her childhood, being raised on her grandmother's farm. She came back to Bedstuy when she was eleven, where she later attended and graduated from Girls' High School, before she went on to receive her bachelor's degree from Brooklyn College. She was a nursery school teacher while also pursuing a master's in elementary education at Columbia University. She started her political career in Brooklyn, working with the Bedford-Stuyvesant Political League and the League of Women Voters, before being elected to the New York State Assembly and eventually the United States Congress, representing New York's Twelfth District.

Shirley Chisholm, of course, did not win the presidency in 1972. She received a small portion of the votes during the Democratic primary, and a sliver of delegates at the convention, but not nearly enough for serious contention. But she had always meant to be a serious candidate. Hers was not a symbolic run at the presidency. It was, however, unsuccessful, and George McGovern secured the Democratic nomination, before being trounced in the popular and electoral vote by the incumbent President Nixon, who resigned in 1974 because of the Watergate scandal.

And so the distinction of being the second president born in New York City goes to Donald Trump. He was born in Queens. No disrespect to Queens; it still has A Tribe Called Quest to call its own. Trump has made his way as a racist real estate developer, a failed casino owner, a failed football team owner, a gossip-page mainstay, a serial abuser, a reality television host, and successful presidential candidate.

There is an alternate timeline, of which I have frequent daydreams, where Shirley Chisholm did win in '72. Except, I have trouble building out a world that's a result of that isolated incident of history. The kind of country that would elect Shirley Chisholm as president would not need Shirley Chisholm to be president. Or rather, it would not view the election of Shirley Chisholm as anything remarkable. It would be a country where being a black woman born to immigrant parents whose first speech on the floor of the House was against the Vietnam War would not be considered a liability in a presidential election. For that to be true, it would need to be a country that did not have a history of antagonism toward black people, women, and immigrants, while also not harboring imperial desires that serve to protect its capitalist regime. That would mean that its founding could not include a class of wealthy white men whose primary concern was ownership and control of the land from which they drew their wealth. And that could have been avoided by respecting the people who were already tending the land when the white men showed up.

Shirley Chisholm was never going to be elected president. Donald Trump was inevitable.

His city of birth rejected him, but New York is, regrettably I'm sure, more responsible for Donald Trump than anywhere else. It is here that his father Fred was able to build and own the more than twenty-seven thousand low-income apartments that generated his wealth, and where he profited off the racial segregation that prompted Woody Guthrie, a

onetime tenant in a Trump property, to write: "I sup-
pose/Old Man Trump knows/Just how much/Racial
Hate/he stirred up/In the bloodpot of human hearts/
When he drawed/That color line/Here at his/Eigh-
teen hundred family project."

And it's in New York City that Donald Trump built
the myth of himself. New York media uncritically ran
with his story about the "small loan" he received from
his father, and then repeated Trump's claims of being
a billionaire without much fact-checking, so long as he
continued to supply dirt on celebrities in his orbit. It's
in New York City that he started slapping his name all
over tasteless buildings and then bragged that his were
the tallest after the World Trade Center towers were
taken down in the attacks of 9/11.

New York enabled him because that's what New
York does. Choose your story, tell it with conviction,
and New York will make room for you. It's here that,
with the right amount of luck, you can live out the
American Dream in whatever way you want.

It's why I, and so many others, came here in the
first place. I wanted to feel as though I belonged somewhere, and my native Virginia wasn't able to accom-
modate me. I wanted the romance of late-night bodega

runs, 2:00 a.m. barhopping, foods and accents from the entire globe within arms' reach, dates at MoMA, art-house films that can't find distribution anywhere else in the country, run-ins with famous people going about their daily lives also in search of anonymity, long subway rides that turn misdirection into discovery, cab rides that open up the skyline, the stars replaced by the city's own light. I wanted every bit of it. I wanted this city to fuel me in the way it had all the writers I admired from afar. I hoped it had enough left for me.

So I left Virginia. For my parents, both born and raised in Washington, DC, during the 1960s and '70s, our Virginia Beach home was their promised land. Our two-story home with a front and backyard on the corner of a cul-de-sac that was zoned for good public schools in a safe and clean environment was all they wanted, for their children certainly, but also for themselves. It was a great deal different from the poverty of their youth, when DC became a practically all-black city, with all the divestment of resources that comes with such a demographic shift, and Chocolate City earned its reputation for danger. As the resources leave, so rises the prevalence of addiction and violence, and where such violence is committed by black people, criminalization follows. My parents' upbringing was defined by all these things, whether directly or by proximity. And so, once they could afford to do so, they left.

They left behind the home their parents hoped would be different from their own homes. My grandparents, born in Virginia and South Carolina, were a part of the wave of black migration up from the southern states to the north in the mid-twentieth century. They were escaping the lives of their parents and grandparents and great-grandparents who had little choice about where they lived, having either themselves been born enslaved or born to those who had been enslaved.

I haven't researched my family history; what little I know is from the research my cousins on my maternal grandmother's side have done. For our fiftieth family reunion they compiled a book of our family story through both my great-grandfather and great-grandmother's lines, as far back as they could trace through documentation, with some family lore thrown in for good measure.

The book begins with Pleasant Lampkins, my great-great-great grandfather and the man whose name my extended family still carries. He was born, enslaved, in 1836 in Mount Airy, North Carolina.

He was owned as property until emancipation at the conclusion of the Civil War in 1865. According to our family's oral history, his former owner gave him a house that previously functioned as a grinding mill. He stayed there for an indeterminate number of years before walking, with his wife, Mollie, the 64.5 miles from Mount Airy to Black Lick, Virginia, for reasons unknown. It was there, in Wythe County, that they raised their children—Alfred, Alamedia, Jonah, John, and Henry, plus Pleasant's two other children, Louis and Susan. Pleasant worked as a day laborer until his death from tuberculosis in June 1912.

Pleasant Lampkins couldn't read or write; six years prior to his birth, a North Carolina statute forbade anyone from teaching him how, and he didn't learn after emancipation. What my family knows of his life comes from scarce documentation, which includes an 1880 census form and his death certificate. There is, therefore, no record of his internal life, no journals to explain his feelings about slavery or emancipation or work or family or white people. I will never know why he walked in the direction he did, why he settled in Wythe County, what he was searching for, if he ever felt fulfilled. In her book *A Field Guide to Getting Lost*, Rebecca Solnit writes:

Getting lost . . . seems like the beginning of finding your way or finding another way, though there are other ways of being lost. Nineteenth-century Americans seldom seem to have gotten lost as disastrously as the strays and corpses picked up by search and rescue teams. I went looking for their tales of being lost and found that being off course for a day or a week wasn't a disaster for those who didn't keep a tight schedule, knew how to live off the land, how to track, how to navigate by heavenly bodies, waterways, and word of mouth in those places before they were mapped.

Pleasant was a nineteenth-century American who found his way but left no record of how and so has not been written into our account of that time. His experience exists outside of what Solnit could have studied. We can take up his cause now, researching and reimagining and revising toward a fuller picture, but Pleasant was one of millions for whom this is true, who existed on this land unable to tell their part of the American story.

I became fixated on Pleasant in part because of what I saw on that death certificate. The first thing to capture my attention was his name: Pleasant, a cruelly ironic name for a person born enslaved. I have only guesses at where the name came from, whether it was a malicious naming on the part of a slave owner (who may have also been his biological father) or an act of hopeful aspiration on the part of parents who were similarly enslaved. There is no way to know, not only because Pleasant could not read and write, but because his parents are unknown. In the places on his death certificate where it asks for "Name of Father," "Birthplace of Father," "Maiden Name of Mother," and "Birthplace of Mother," there is cursive handwriting that says "Unknown." It is certified "to the best of my knowledge" by his daughter Susan.

It's true, in some sense, that we all start with an unknown, but here is mine and my family's written down, a reminder of what the violence of slavery has taken away from us. Pleasant Lampkins was unable to know or say from whom and where he came. And so my own history can only start with him.

The book my cousins compiled features others, and some even a bit further back than Pleasant, but the other reason I became fixated on him is that on the page next to his death certificate is a picture of him, taken sometime between 1910 and 1912, when he would have been around seventy-five years old.

It's as blurry as you might imagine, but I can see him there, standing between two horses, one black and one white, sporting a wide-brimmed hat, a long jacket, and possibly overalls. He doesn't appear to have any facial hair, though maybe what I'm thinking of as shadows are patches of black hair that survived aging. It's difficult to tell whether his eyes are closed or if the picture has simply deteriorated too much to make out much of anything. I wouldn't immediately say that he looks like anyone I know. But there he is, born enslaved to the unknown, the man whose name was my grandmother's until she married. I am because of him and the choices he made. He did not run away; he was enslaved until he was emancipated. He did not stay in his native North Carolina; he moved 64.5 miles away for reasons I will never know. He raised a family in Wythe County, which my grandmother then left for DC, which my parents then left for Virginia Beach, which I left for New York City, all of us hoping that somewhere along this way there is something better than what was given to us.

Pleasant could have kept walking, I suppose, if he thought there would be something better beyond Virginia. He could have kept on to New York City.

But in 1741, New Yorkers hanged sixteen enslaved black people, burned thirteen others at the stake, and deported seventy more on suspicion of an insurrection. The last of New York's enslaved were not freed until 1827, nine years before Pleasant was born. In 1863, during the Draft Riots, Irish mobs burned down the Colored Orphan Asylum, after turning a legitimate gripe about the rich being able to avoid conscription into the war into violence against the black population that simply wanted to live free. In 1867, two years after the end of the Civil War, Mark Twain described New York City as "a splendid desert—a domed and steepled solitude, where the stranger is lonely in the midst of a million of his race." Whether Pleasant was aware of any of this, again, I will never know, but I do know that wherever we go, there we are, and no matter how far Pleasant walked, he would not have escaped the thing that had so defined his existence. It is what makes this country.

But I did come here, believing there would be something different. I know better, but stubbornly held onto the delusion anyway. I wanted the romance of New York City, but I moved to the same place that killed Eleanor Bumpurs and Amadou Diallo. I moved to a city of slumlords getting rich off rising rents and displacing poor families. I moved to a place that would rather allow a world-renowned public transportation system crumble than raise taxes on the rich to pay to improve it and therefore improve the lives of the millions who depend on it. I came to the birthplace of broken windows policing. I moved to a city that has more unoccupied homes than it does homeless people and yet won't fix its "homeless problem."

The city is, obviously, more than this, but it is this too. It was once a trading outpost for the Dutch empire and grew into an international hub of media/culture/politics/finance, and it is still all those things that crush those who are subjected to its dominance rather than participating in it.

Our fiftieth family reunion took place Labor Day weekend of 2016 in Max Meadows, Virginia. A few weeks later, back in New York, I stopped into a tattoo parlor and got "1836" tattooed on the inside of my left wrist. It didn't heal properly, likely because I was sloppy with the aftercare process, having grown a bit arrogant with it being my ninth tattoo. But it's perhaps fitting that this scar I've chosen to represent those whom no one would have didn't heal the way it should. I say that I got it to honor Pleasant, but the more I consider it, I think I got it because I had run away from Pleasant, without even knowing him. It's easy, when this city opens up to you, to be seduced by its undeniable charm, and then to forget the other parts of it exist. It's preferable, even, when you spend time thinking, researching, writing, and talking about the worst of this country, the worst of our humanity, to pretend that the cocktail parties and advance press screenings and galas and penthouses you start to get invited to are actually what make this city, this life. Who wouldn't choose that, particularly when the alternative is the precarity of a body you didn't choose?

But I look down at my wrist and recall that I could only tattoo the year Pleasant was born because his date of birth is also an unknown. (Whether or not he ever chose a date to celebrate his birth is something else I'll never know; did he view life as something worth celebrating?) And I look at the year, 1836, and remember that he was maybe twenty-nine years old when he could call himself free, the same age I was when I decided to put this number on my wrist permanently. It is a reminder that I didn't just happen—I am a product of the time and circumstances that made Pleasant Lampkins an American slave. And what made Pleasant is still with us all.

Choosing a new story cannot mean denying the old one. Doing so only leaves you with delusions of your own making.

Donald Trump is what happens when you choose the lie. He is the embodiment of the American delusion. He changes his story based on what he wants to be true rather than what is. He has rewritten his history to flatter himself and no matter what evidence he is presented with—even if they are his own words—he retells the flattering lie until it is accepted as a plausible narrative. His detractors are attacked, disparaged, demeaned, and threatened until they are either crushed by the pressure or so delegitimized that no public takes their claims seriously enough.

Whatever else he is, Trump is an American creation, and he was produced in the part of America that believes itself to be exempt from what it views as backward ideologies that prevail elsewhere. But he is New York City's homegrown.

Shirley Chisholm was too, and this is what makes me believe, perhaps foolheartedly, that the potential for a meaningful insurgency exists within us, it simply isn't being nurtured in the way it needs to be. Here I'm back to my daydreams of Chisholm winning in '72 and telling the country the truth of itself. It still isn't prepared to hear it.

Only when I daydream like this, I catch myself hating the thought that Chisholm would have needed to be president for these truths to resonate. It tells me that I've bought in to the thinking that turns the president into a messiah capable of saving the wretched from themselves. As a country, we obsess over the election of one person who is a part of one branch of our federal government, and we ask for a democratic outcome from an anti-democratic process so that we can feel pleased with ourselves for having chosen the one person responsible for ensuring we do not descend into chaos. Then we are left to panic when the country has chosen wrong.

This is why I cringe when I hear the open pining for Alexandria Ocasio-Cortez to someday run for president (or the bemoaning of the fact that she is constitutionally barred from doing so at present). Her surprise primary win and election to the US Congress out of New York's Fourteenth District provided a glimmer of hope as the darkness of the Trump administration had made quick work in suppressing the will to fight back in many Americans. Bright, young, charismatic, with a moral clarity that stood in direct opposition to what we were receiving from the White House, Ocasio-Cortez excited people eager for a win. She drew comparisons to Shirley Chisholm because she took on the Democratic party machine in New York City and won, and for her outspoken character, pulling few punches in speaking to the urgency of the issues at hand.

A key difference is that Ocasio-Cortez's political home was the Democratic Socialists of America, the country's largest socialist organization that had seen a surge in membership in the wake of the 2016 election. Not that Chisholm's politics were not, especially when compared to those of her contemporaries in Congress, radical and largely concerned with the ways in which we could alleviate the oppressive nature of poverty, but it is something else entirely to name an ideological opposition to the prevailing American doctrine of capitalism. Such an alignment orders her politics, such that Ocasio-Cortez provides an anti-capitalist framework for understanding issues of racial justice, gender justice, and climate justice, while also not losing sight of the particulars of each of these struggles.

Some of this has been lost in her celebrity, which was to be expected; focusing on her personality rather than her ideas is a way of acknowledging her popularity while neutralizing those ideas. Repeating her story as the rise from bartender to Congress member reassures everyone that the American Dream remains possible, even as Ocasio-Cortez, in her policies and in each of her critiques of DC politicking and Trump, calls it into question.

But the point of Ocasio-Cortez's story should not be more exceptionalism, more mythmaking. It should, rather, point us toward the strength of movements, to recognize the need for collective action to defeat entrenched power. Ocasio-Cortez did not emerge as a phoenix, mighty and solo—years prior, people were laughed at for occupying Wall Street, then chastised for supporting what was deemed an unserious presidential campaign, before they joined a nearly disappeared socialist organization whose resurgence incubated the Ocasio-Cortez congressional run. This is the strength of people acting in solidarity and not sitting idle in anticipation of the arrival of a savior. "Strong people don't need strong leaders," Ella Baker's words call out to us from the past. Our preoccupation cannot be with how to make Ocasio-Cortez president but with how we fill the halls of power with all the Ocasio-Cortezes waiting in the wings.

Of course, as it stands, the ideas Ocasio-Cortez fights for would resonate more with the American people if she were president. The president wields so much influence that we are caught in a conundrum of where to place our political energy: to ignore the presidency would be a huge tactical mistake, but it consumes so much of our attention that to adequately counter its influence can exhaust our touchstone resources of time and energy.

But the presidency holds this influence precisely because we invest so little in constructing our bonds of collective power and community outside of the office. Our time is constricted, of course, by the need to find ways to survive under late capitalism where our capacity to care for ourselves dwindles by the second, as a ruling class hoards capital and extracts more labor from us for less compensation. We are left without the energy—physically, mentally, and emotionally—needed to participate in an actual democracy.

And so we become content to hand over the reins of decision-making to one person, who we exceptionalize out of necessity, because we must believe this person is the most deserving caretaker of our national present and future. They must be a worthy heir to the myth.

Shirley Chisholm was never going to be president because she sought to shatter the myth. It's unfortunate in some respects that she never got the chance, but I also know it would take more than one presidency to do such work. And had she been elected, there would likely have been a backlash, as we are seeing now and have experienced throughout this country's history, that would work one hundred times harder to recast her as a villain to the American identity. And anyway, she didn't need to be president. What she actually needed was more people to stand with her. That is the only real value of running for president, the visibility it affords you to go about building a coalition around your ideas. But it shouldn't be the case that you must run for president to achieve that.

When I discuss my disdain for presidential politics with my friend Natasha, she nearly always quotes from one of her favorite poems, "Of Being Numerous" by George Oppen: "It is the air of atrocity/An event as ordinary/As a President." If only the election of a president were a more mundane affair. But what Oppen gets at is that the name and face and party affiliation of the president may change, but the presidency itself is beholden to a narrow corridor of ideas. The presidency is marked by that which is comfortable and unthreatening to the American identity or its hierarchies of power. The degree of variance at times may feel like genuine progress, but what persists is the ideology of America that allows for only so much change before reverting back in on itself.

This will happen so long as the fear of loss triumphs over a desire for justice and accountability. A nation unwilling to tell the truth about itself to itself will circle its delusions until there is nothing left to tether it to reality. And then ...

———

UNDOUBTEDLY, WHEN THE STATUE OF SHIRLEY Chisholm is unveiled at Prospect Park, I will walk by it and have an emotional reaction. There are so few statues honoring women in this city, and this one is a part of a larger project to build more. I will look at the statue and think of what could have been, catch myself thinking such frivolous thoughts, and then be angry all over again. I'll remember the man who set up his makeshift shelter outside the train station across the street and wonder what happened to him. I will imagine the people who will sleep near Chisholm's statue and have the police called on them. I will think about how in a few years hardly anyone who looks like Shirley Chisholm, or shares her Caribbean background, will be living near her statue. I will go about my day.

But then perhaps I will remember that Shirley Chisholm voluntarily stepped away from it all. Mostly, anyway. Her husband was sick and she wanted to care for him, but she had also grown disillusioned with her liberal colleagues who reacted poorly to the Reagan Revolution, and she decided it was not worth it to have to fight the opposition and those purportedly on her side who were turning further away from their stated principles. Her congressional career didn't end as she had previously believed it would, ousted by a power greater than herself because she refused to be silent on issues that mattered. She walked away, having been elected and then reelected six times by the voters in her district. In 1983, she went on to teach sociology and politics at Mount Holyoke College for several years, then helped form the reproductive rights organization African-American Women for Reproductive Freedom in 1990, then retired to Florida. She passed away in 2005.

But seven times she showed up for the voters in the Twelfth Congressional District of New York, "unbought and unbossed," and the voters chose her until she chose not to do it anymore. It may have just been a little pocket of Brooklyn, where the dispossessed and marginalized had been pushed to live, but they made the best of what they had. And they mattered. They showed that the potential is there.

Electoral politics is not the end-all be-all of political participation. It isn't particularly radical and really only serves as a measure of how much of a shift has occurred as a result of multiple levels of organizing that take place away from the voting booth. Gil Scott-Heron became famous for writing "The Revolution Will Not Be Televised," and like so many things that become a small piece of a monoculture, his messaging has been misunderstood. He meant that the revolution is not what you see happening before you; what you see is a result of the revolution that has already taken place. Marcuse argued that a true revolution is a totalizing affair, that it is not possible for a revolution to take place in one aspect of society without revolution overtaking *every* aspect of that society. This is both an acknowledgment of the interlocking structures of oppression that order our lives and a narrowing of the definition of the word *revolution* itself. According to Marcuse's definition, revolution should be reserved for total change, the construction of an entirely new world.

If we take this as true, it requires what Gil Scott-Heron was pointing toward: an inner revolution that changes the way we think about the world we inhabit and the people we exist alongside. "Thoughts afford the sole method of escape from purely impulsive or purely routine action," the philosopher John Dewey wrote in *How We Think*. Our thoughts have, thus far, been ordered by a world beset with inequality on all fronts. Our impulses are influenced by the ways in which we have been socialized, and our routines are those that serve to reinforce our national delusions. Confrontation with this way of thinking is a prerequisite for revolution.

Dewey, again:

Thinking begins in what may fairly enough be called a *forked-road* situation, a situation which is ambiguous, which presents a dilemma, which proposes alternatives. As long as our activity glides smoothly along from one thing to another, or as long as we permit our imagination to entertain fancies at pleasure, there is no call for reflection. Difficulty or obstruction in the way of reaching a belief brings us, however, to a pause. In the suspense of uncertainty, we metaphorically climb a tree.

The history of the United States, like that of humanity itself, is a series of "forked-road" situations, of which Donald Trump is the latest. Our problem has been that we generally approach the uncertainty produced by such situations without much reflection; we climb Dewey's metaphorical tree and survey the alternatives without being intentional in selecting our new path. More often than not, we choose that which is most familiar to us, or else, when we do choose something new, we bring too much of our old selves with us for it to constitute a revolution. It happened in our founding, where the "revolution" to break away from tyrannical Britain still meant the imposition of tyranny against all who were not white, land-owning men; it happened again with the failure of Reconstruction, where the country could have atoned for its "original sin" but instead supported a resurgent white supremacy; the Great Depression should have been a time for restructuring our economy so as to strengthen workers' unions and ensure that such a concentration of wealth never occurred again, but instead it found a way to save capitalism by providing it with a mask of gentility. The women's movement and sexual "revolution," gay liberation, the disability rights movement . . . each of these uprisings provided opportunity for Americans to examine ourselves, to question our core beliefs, and to change—to fulfill the promise of a true revolution.

We have convinced ourselves we do not require revolution. There is something ingrained in the American character, we say to ourselves, that will, no matter what obstacles we are faced with, endure, prevail, and prove victorious.

But what have we won? Our reward for believing in the indomitable American spirit is the presidency of Donald Trump, which has only exposed our national fragility. We are a country that can be taken by a known grifter so long as he speaks the language of our delusions.

During his first year as president, I noticed that there were never any papers on Donald Trump's desk. I don't assume the country would be better off if there had been, but image is everything to him, and an empty desk does not look the part of a president at work. Every president before him has been photographed sitting studiously at the Oval Office desk overrun with documents. It may be stagecraft, but it is considered stagecraft. It signals to the American people the immense burden their president has taken up on their behalf. *Look at all those papers—how could he ever read them all?* They are, undoubtedly, full of important information about the economy, terrorism, and other items of significance that only an American president should be trusted with understanding. We can rest well knowing that he is in control.

Trump has spent his entire four-decade public career mastering the art of manipulating public perception, and yet felt no need to take the small step of having his desk photographed with a smattering of folders and papers spread across it, as though he is a real president. It's rather lazy, but he can afford to be. The other presidents have, frankly, done too much. Americans are eager to be deceived.

I suppose I should appreciate that Trump is a historically unpopular president. Perhaps I am denying the American people some due credit and the desire for deception does not run as deep as a cynical read projects.

But I am not soothed by the unpopularity of Trump when I also see the concurrent popularity of that which made Trump. I don't mean the explicit expressions of white nationalism and misogyny, though it's clearly troubling how popular those remain. I mean the thing that produced "protest" signs that suggested protest would not have been necessary if Clinton had won, the same thing that produced presidential candidates promising a return to the glory days of Obama. It's the thing that caused Abraham Lincoln to say in his first inaugural address, on the eve of the country's most deadly and consequential war: "We are not enemies, but friends. We must not be enemies. Though passion may have strained, it must not break our bonds of affection. The mystic chords of memory, stretching from every battlefield and patriot grave to every living heart and hearthstone all over this broad land, will yet swell the chorus of the Union, when again touched, as surely they will be, by the better angels of our nature."

This thing, whether rendered crudely or poetically, is the misguided belief that America's history possesses something better to which we can return.

But it is not there. We have not been friends, but competitors. We have not practiced affection—at our absolute best we manage tolerance. We silence our better angels before turning them into familiar devils.

This is not our fate, but it has been our choice. We can, and must, begin to choose differently, in every way. We must choose revolution, reminded as we are by Hannah Arendt in *On Revolution*, that the aim of revolution has always been freedom. We cannot claim to love freedom if we are not willing to change in order to achieve it. The American inclination has been to define freedom on individual terms. But freedom is a collective project under which we form the bonds of community and build the infrastructure necessary to ensure survival and prosperity. Freedom cannot be reduced to walking from the plantation in North Carolina to a small town in Virginia if the rest of that life offers no path toward self-actualization. Freedom should not make your home something you feel the need to escape in order to have a chance for yourself and your family. Freedom should not be subject to the whims of the market. It should not require luck.

Freedom must mean that we believe our collective future is possible through our own actions, in solidarity with one another, because we know that we are all we got.

"We are not powerless," poet and essayist June Jordan wrote in *Some of Us Did Not Die*. "We are indispensable despite all atrocities of state and corporate policy to the contrary. At a minimum we have the power to stop cooperating with our enemies." And we can do so even when the enemy exists within us.

———————

THE CONCEPT FOR DE LA SOUL'S MUSIC VIDEO FOR its 1996 single "Stakes Is High," the leadoff for the album of the same name, is fairly simple. The three members of the group, as well as some associates, are mostly pictured in everyday situations—doing laundry, washing the car, hanging out at the basketball court—while every once in a while the video cuts to one of them rapping underneath a New York City bridge. The visuals don't appear to match the big energy of the beat or the urgency of Posdnuos and Dave's delivery, until you account for the chaos that is New York City itself providing the backdrop. This is the point: at any given moment, underneath the mundane lurks an emergency.

One part of the video that stands apart from this messaging is where Posdnuos plays a game of one-on-one with then–Philadelphia 76ers rookie Jerry Stackhouse. Posdnuos is wearing a black Michael Jordan/Chicago Bulls jersey. The two face off at center court, Stackhouse, at six feet six, towering over the much shorter Posdnuos. And yet, Posdnuos takes the taller professional basketball player off the dribble, then the camera cuts to an image of him driving toward the basket unimpeded, suggesting he has left Stackhouse behind, before he soars to dunk.

It's an all-around fantasy—Posdnuos isn't nearly tall enough to dunk, nor does he possess greater athleticism than a professional ball player five years his junior. But it's the kind of fantasy one can indulge when they are in charge of writing their own story. It does not line up with the rest of De La's reality-based video, but it's a moment to cut loose and daydream about what you wish could be.

In this way, when myth is engaged as myth, it does not carry the same dangers I've stressed. Myth can be where the imagination flourishes, where we tell stories about our ideal world. Such stories can contain the values we wish to uphold, the principles we believe must guide us, and the moral clarity to build systems that center empathy, care, justice, and equality. Without this imagining, there is no revolution.

Where America has fucked up is by telling the myth as history—pretending that who we want to be is who we have always been—then building a proud and belligerent national identity out of the myth. American myths obscure a shameful past and protect the powerful. De La's myth is clear fantasy and unachievable. But myth can project forward. It can set the bar for us to reach. It may initially appear fantastical, unattainable even, but given its proper place, myth can provide us a blueprint for thinking outside the limitations of the present and allow us to imagine a future that is not dictated by the flaws of our history.

But unchecked, myth written as history can continue to inflict harm. In her memoir, *The Yellow House*, Sarah M. Broom writes of her native New Orleans and the effect the repetition of these myths has on the people who live under them:

> The mythology of New Orleans—that it is always the place for a good time; that its citizens are the happiest people alive, willing to smile, dance, cook, and entertain for you; that it is a progressive city open to whimsy and change—can sometimes suffocate the people who live and suffer under the place's burden, burying them within layers and layers of signifiers, making it impossible to truly get at what is dysfunctional about the city. . . . A city where being held up while getting out of your car is the norm, where many children graduate school without

knowing how to spell, where neglected communities exist everywhere, sometimes a stone's throw from overabundance.

"When you come from a mythologized place, as I do," Broom writes, "who are you in that story?"

It depends. Sometimes you're the *I*, others the *we*, or the *they*, or the *you*. Where you place yourself will be determined by how honest you are willing to be about your role in the story.

One thing is certain—you are never too far from being part of *us*. No matter the divisions that have been created, as human beings we continue to rely on one another to help make meaning out of our random existence. We are bonded; we are us. That is the only constant; it is the only place where we can always return. It's messy and unpredictable, but also the only place from which we can determine the future. Stakes is high, and what little time we have left can no longer be spent on preserving our mythical selves. We must be willing to lose our old story. We must choose us.

THE AFTERTHOUGHT

But I who am bound by my mirror/as well as my bed/see causes in colour/as well as sex/and sit here wondering/which me will survive/all these liberations.

—Audre Lorde,
"Who Said It Was Simple"

The other side of E. B. White's observation that "no one should come to New York to live unless he is willing to be lucky" is that you must also be willing to be unlucky, or otherwise have the means to survive being unlucky. I do not come from such means. Due in part to my father's twenty-year military career, my family was ostensibly middle class, the first generation on either side to have such a distinction. On the surface, it sounds like a fulfillment of the American Dream, but being black and middle class holds little of the freedom promised in that status, especially when you are the first. The responsibility of care for family, immediate and extended, and friends, close and distant, falls on the financial resources that under other circumstances would have been thought of as extra. This added strain is not just financial but psychological, as it places more pressure to work harder and longer to provide for everyone within your orbit. They are depending on your access to the Dream for their survival.

Our comfort was precarious. Subjected to the ebbs and flows of capitalism, with no prior wealth on which to rely, the line between striving for and achieving the American Dream remained blurred. It was never certain if we were coming or going, until it was abundantly clear.

I moved to New York City knowing there was no familial safety net to catch me. I moved here while making less than a living wage, under the romantic notion that New York City offered the kind of freedom I grew up believing in. I'm still here now because I've been just lucky enough. Whenever I say this, some well-meaning person interjects and suggests that I not downplay my own hard work or talent, wanting to reassure me that what they see as my success is no fluke, that I made this happen by dint of my own determination and diligence. I try to appreciate their earnest consideration of my self-esteem, but I have known hard work, I see hard work every day, and hard work is a guarantee of nothing except more hard work. Unless it kills you.

Hard work is not in and of itself virtuous, though the unofficial American credo would have us believe otherwise. But convincing people that hard work is its own reward is a prime tool in the arsenal deployed by the capitalist class to ensure they never have to relinquish their ill-gotten wealth. They convince others that they already have their share.

I am not, obviously, the first person to ever poke holes in the idea that is the American Dream, but no matter how many times you have heard it before, no matter how many times you have heard it critiqued, I believe it bears repeating: the American Dream is bullshit. And it's not bullshit so much because of its relative unlikelihood, but because it rests on the very idea that inequality is natural and good. You can, in America, come from nothing and gain everything—a fantastic idea if you think it is at all just that there would be people who have nothing. The Dream is premised on the idea that someone, somewhere, will always have so little that they must do more, must sacrifice their time, their body, their values, their self in order to achieve, in order to have more. And more is not always more, sometimes more is simply the basic means of survival. Most of the time.

Believing that it is the only path to a better life, generation after generation has fought and strived to have greater access to the American Dream and rarely stepped back to ask if it was something worth having. There is an aphorism, "Pressure makes diamonds," but for the aphorism to be meaningful, you must find value in diamonds. But diamonds are little more than shiny rocks. Are they worth the pressure?

Is the American Dream worth it? I think, reader, we both know my answer. But I ask you to consider the question, and all it entails, for yourself. Is the potential for the American Dream worth enduring the brutality of American Life?

Perhaps, seeing it worded this way, with the positive connotations of the phrase "American Dream" still tapping around your head, your answer remains yes, so I will ask it another way: Is Donald Trump worth it?

Because Donald Trump is the inevitable result of holding tight to the American Dream. He was inevitable in 2016 and, barring a revolutionary turn for this country, he will be inevitable again in our future. He is the end result of allowing the delusion about our history, of uninterrogated whiteness and masculinity, of making freedom synonymous with capitalist accumulation, of unearned arrogance and untempered individual ambition . . . He is all the things that create American culture, whether they are acknowledged or not.

The failure to acknowledge these core facets of American identity for what they are before 2016 allowed Trump to win the presidential election. His win has produced enough of an existential crisis among the electorate that it is possible he could lose in 2020, though the Electoral College still works in his favor. But defeating Trump is not the most important political goal facing us, only the most immediate. To prevent another Trump requires a reckoning Americans have never exhibited the stomach for.

It has certainly been true for those among us with the reach and influence to set the framework for what issues we discuss and how we do so. Select members of the media still struggle to identify his rhetoric and behavior as racist, as if doing so would taint their credibility as unbiased observers of the state. But it is precisely their refusal to call him, his actions, his policies racist that diminishes their credibility, not only because it is an abdication of their moral duty, but because it is a failure of their professional duty as well. How can the fourth estate hold people in power accountable if it will not name the type of power being wielded?

Perhaps they don't believe it will matter once Trump is no longer in office because they make the mistake of believing he is a deviation from the norm, rather than a full expression of America's basest desires, and that

American institutions are equipped to eject him, rather than accepting that those institutions are founded on and continue to foster the ideological grounds upon which Trump has been able to feed. Perhaps their purportedly unbiased observation begins with a bias toward the American myth and it has yet to course correct.

We have all done it, played a part in the maintenance of the myth, to varying degrees, so this is not an indictment specific to those select media members. But it is worth asking what the prospects for untangling the myth are when the people who are meant to have the most close-up view of our society cannot see it for what it is. What questions go unasked, what ideas go unexplored?

I pursued writing because I believed something that I struggle to believe now, which is that the written word has revolutionary potential. I believed in the purity of writing as a vessel for truth, and perhaps more foolishly I believed in people's yearning for said truth. I believed the truth would always win and all that was necessary was to say it.

It didn't take much to disabuse me of my naivete regarding the truth—a brief brush with the comments section of anything published on the internet lets you know people will fight for their perceived reality at all costs, even (or maybe especially) when it is not rooted in provable facts. It is more recently that I have viewed the written word as increasingly futile. It is difficult to think it is useful to write more words into the constantly churning content mill while children languish in concentration camps at the border (and, as I revise, the fear and death we face with the COVID-19 pandemic). Does winning the argument over their nomenclature actually help? Do more words serve a purpose when reality is being shaped by people who don't care to read anything?

The longer I sit in front of blank pages that demand more words, the more I think to myself that I should be charging the camps to physically free those imprisoned for daring to threaten the fragility of white identity. I would most assuredly be shot, but is it not a cause worth being shot over? Doesn't the situation demand more urgency, more throwing caution to the wind? Are the stakes high or not?

I feel the depths of my own uselessness in those times when I am thinking most like an American—that is, when I am thinking that the responsibility of societal transformation falls on a single, messiah-like figure. In my fantasies, I could be such a figure.

It's an uncomfortable thought when you realize you share this fascistic impulse with Donald Trump, who swore he and he alone could rescue America, return it to glory. Different aims, to be sure, but it is a shared dismissal of community in favor of a narcissistic desire to be adored for an impossible heroism.

Worse is how such fantasies distract from the work that can be done. The written word still matters, but only insofar as the writer has considered whom they are writing to and why. The revolutionary potential of the written word lies less in the dictum "Speak truth to power" than it does in gathering the power of the disaffected.

Since 1865, *torcedores* (cigar rollers) in Cuba's cigar factories have gone about their work while *lectores* (readers) read to them, from newspapers, novels, and other available literature. Aside from breaking up the tedium of their labor, lectores afforded torcedores an opportunity to engage with culture while still earning their wages (in turn, the torcedores paid a portion of their wages to the lectores, which eventually became a full-time position). Additionally, with the reading of more politicized material, the practice helped to activate and organize the workers, and because of this,

Cuba's cigar rollers assisted in the fight to win independence from Spain.

Everyone has a role to play; it's a matter of whether or not you step into it. I didn't intend to write this book. At the exact moment Donald Trump was placing his hand on the Bible and swearing to uphold the oath of office, my editor and I were in a pizza place in Bushwick discussing an altogether different idea, one that would not require us to think about the impending "Trump era." The last thing I wanted to do was write anything else that would prompt white people to ask me how to cure racism—though I've come to believe that is the only question they care to ever ask black thinkers. I had decided I would write a book that meant devoting my time to researching things that were wholly unrelated to the news cycle or Trump's consistent obnoxiousness. When we left the restaurant, we had happily settled on an idea that would allow me an escape.

Except when I sat down to work on that book, the very first sentence I wrote had Trump's name in it. I refreshed Twitter every few minutes under the irrational belief that so long as I had a minute-to-minute update on the state of the world, then nothing truly catastrophic could happen.

Writing into the anxiety was not something I wanted, but a responsibility I knew I had. My role is to write words and hope they land where they are useful. I can no more predict the impact of my work than I can lottery numbers or NBA free agency. All I want is to be able to look back and say that I did my part, and I did it to the best of my abilities. I hope we can all say the same.

———

I WROTE, SCRAPPED, REWROTE, AND EDITED THIS book through what I now see as a prolonged depression. I have dealt with depression since I was about twelve years old, and I like to think I have become good at recognizing the signs and warding off the worst of its effects. I can, under what are relatively normal circumstances for me, note the change in my sleep habits, acknowledge my social withdrawal, and upon realizing I have slipped deeper into an overwhelming sadness, correct some very basic things in my life (diet, exercise, sleep) that allow me to get in touch with the root cause of my depression and seek out useful solutions. This is how I have made peace with its presence.

For the duration of the Trump presidency, I have found this does not work. This book has been an attempt to argue that this moment in American history is not an aberration, that it is the course this country has always been on because the power of the narrative we have all contributed to has propelled us here. If I didn't believe that, I would not have spent so much time trying to convince you of it.

But it is also true that I see this time and its particular frightfulness. The planet is burning and the people with the power to prevent that from happening would rather watch it burn than give up their inflated status. They will lock children in cages, leave them susceptible to assault and famine and disease, all to protect the wealth they have amassed through the theft of white supremacist patriarchal capitalism. And as the clock runs out on our time to save our species from complete, self-inflicted, total annihilation, I feel more powerless than ever to do anything to stop it.

The circumstances of my depression are no longer "normal." This has not been a case of uncovering repressed trauma that needs to be addressed, or shifting from survival tactics that have outworn their practical usefulness. This prolonged depression has its roots in the creeping sense that we could be living through the end—that we will be the last humans, and we will not have done nearly enough to fight for our survival.

I am scared. That is as plain as I can say it. I am afraid every single day. When I finished writing my first book, a strange optimism washed over me. There was, of course, the euphoria of the accomplishment itself, but there was also a genuine belief that its existence proved there was a path toward something better. I wrote about the interior lives of black men in America and felt, truly felt, there may be some shift coming whereby black men would be given space to examine their existence, work their way out of complicity in destructive systems, and heal. The notes I received after the book's publication only strengthened that belief.

I had my sense of the possible shattered on November 8, 2016. I did not previously believe that in my lifetime we would defeat the entrenched forces of white supremacist heteropatriarchal capitalism, but I had come around to believing that a slow, frustrating, but ultimately sustainable victory was something my friends' children may someday experience, plus all the jubilation that would come along with it. That changed. I broke on that day, two days after my thirtieth birthday, outside a bar in San Francisco. I broke and I have not recovered.

Yet here I am, writing to you, reader, telling you what I hope you already know, already feel, or if you don't, I hope I can convince you to feel alongside me: stakes is high. They have never been higher. Our very survival is on the line. And I am writing not just to convince you that stakes is high but that something *can* be done about it. Revolution must be swift and uncompromising; it will be scary and potentially violent. Before it can be any of those things, it must be thought of as possible. It must be a meaningful political stance that we take, to believe our future is worth the fight, worth the sacrifice. It will require our radical honesty about who we have been, who we are now, and the courage to move past the discomfort of such honesty toward the tremendous task of building a future worthy of our best ideals. It will ask us to have faith.

My friend Jesse, who in stark contrast to me found resolve after the 2016 election, reminds me often of an important lesson he has learned in his work: all organizing is faith-based organizing, as you must believe that what you are asking people to do is possible against all evidence to the contrary. But I am not an organizer. As a writer, I have always started from a position of more skepticism and less conviction. That has made this book difficult to write. I don't wish to leave you, or myself, with a doomed outlook. I want to regain a sense of possibility.

I have tried to find it in pockets: the teenagers who lead climate marches, the protests at the border against family separation, the defeat of new prison construction, the ending of cash bail, a tide of progressive lawmakers elected to local and national offices. I have tried.

But then I can walk by the Planned Parenthood in New York City and watch a person affix a cross to the side of the building and pray over it and become undone again. I feel fragile.

This book, then, is not just a polemical indictment of the American Dream, or an intervention in the public discourse regarding our political priorities, or even a clarion call for revolution. It is, at its core, a desperate plea for community. I want to shake loose the dread, and I know that I cannot do it alone.

But I also cannot do it with the American myth hanging overhead. Empires fall. Nations end. The United States will not be any exception. What does not have to end is our commitment to one another.

"America leads the world in shocks," Gil Scott-Heron said. "Unfortunately, America does not lead the world in deciphering the cause of shock."

Donald Trump was a shock. The causes are not unknowable. Deciphering them requires an abundance of honesty. People much smarter than me have developed more grounded strategies for what this change looks like in practical terms. I am only here to convince you of the necessity of such change and urge you to set aside the fear of loss in favor of the imagination of our next world. Imagining where we want to go teaches us how to get there.

No one ever said it would be simple, only that it is possible.

Acknowledgments

I Gotta Say What Up!!!

First and foremost to Katy O'Donnell, the best and most patient editor in the entire world. I told her this book would be done a million different times . . . she knew I was lying and stuck with me anyway. She took this vague idea and molded it into the book you've just read (or, if you're like me, are about to read after you've looked at the acknowledgments) by pushing me to think harder and write clearer than I have ever. No one gets me like she does.

And Jessica Papin, my equally patient agent, my biggest advocate, the guide to my career for so long now. She's so dedicated to making this work that she sent me a whole box of Oreos to snack on while getting this book done. It was the most crucial act of this entire process.

Oh, and I have to thank Chris Juby and Emily Lavelle, who did publicity on my last book. I didn't get a chance to thank them in those acknowledgments, but they are the reason anyone heard of *Invisible Man, Got the Whole World Watching*. I owe them more than I can put into words here (not, like, royalties or anything, but just more).

Brooke Parsons! My current publicist! I'm so at ease knowing she's on the case. I'm always anxious, to be clear, but Brooke is a calming presence. She thinks steps ahead of anything I'm ever worried about.

Kenrya Rankin gets a major shout-out because copyediting is so important and she definitely helped polish some things that needed a spit shine.

Melissa Veronesi (another very patient person . . . I have to do better with making all these people wait on me) who managed everything in production that turned my Google doc into an actual book. That work cannot go unrecognized.

Grateful for Lindsay Fradkoff and Miguel Cervantes whose jobs in marketing are so crucial and I admit to not fully understanding.

Taya Kitman continues to hold me down at the newly revamped Type Media Center. Her support has meant everything to me these last . . . seven? Eight years? I am getting old. Thank you for getting me to old age, Taya.

Carmel Lobello listened to me read this entire book out loud, so I could catch any mistakes before it was finalized. Not sure what makes a person be that kind, but very glad she is.

Kiese Laymon. Kiese Laymon. Kiese Laymon. He literally saved my life. In the literal sense of the word literally. I love him as a writer and even more as a human.

And Nicole Cliffe! A guardian angel!

Alana Levinson came through with some clutch words of encouragement at a difficult point of the first draft stage.

I've worked with some really great editors since the last book came out who helped me push myself as a writer and produce some work that informed my approach this time around, and I'm forever in their debt. Extra special thanks to Rachel Poser, Eliza Borné, Laura Marsh, Ryan Dombal, and Chris Gayomali.

Gotta say what up to my ultimate party partner and one of the best writers in the world, Tracy O'Neill.

And to the whole world of whiskey reviewers who exist on YouTube and served as my procrastination material for incredibly long stretches . . . but I learned a lot! And to bourbon. Just bourbon itself.

Always The Teenage Mutant Ninja Turtles. Always them.

I bet at this point they think I was going to leave them out, but there's no chance: JESSE MYERSON, MOLLY KNEFEL, JOHN KNEFEL, GIDEON OLIVER, NATASHA LENNARD, LUKAS HERMSMEIER, RYAN DEVEREAUX, ANDREA JONES, ALI GHARIB, NICK PINTO, HANNAH COHEN, ABBY ELLIS, MAE SMITH—I LOVE YOU ALL.

And for sure those two little ones, Freddie and Zelda.

Carina del Valle Schorske heard the idea for this book before it was even a proposal and remains better at explaining my ideas than I am.

Can't forget *Avengers: Endgame* because for reasons I can't really explain it was the only thing that helped me write during that home stretch, and therefore I have watched the entire three-hour film *several* times over.

For everyone who got the first book (however you came across it) and has high hopes for this one, I hope I didn't let you down.

To anybody coming into contact with my work for the first time via this book: abolish the police. If you take nothing else away from this, take that.

I'm so thankful for all the writers, too numerous to name, that have made work that has made mine possible. When I question the meaning of all this, I remember you and what your work has meant to the world. You make it all make sense. You make me feel less lonely.

If I didn't mention you this time, check back to the first book's acknowledgments, I'm almost certain you're in there. If not, I'm sorry and drinks on me next time.

And last but not least, to everyone who has spent their lives being considered last and treated like the least: it's time. We all we got.

We all we got.

Credit: Syreeta McFadden

Mychal Denzel Smith is the author of the *New York Times* bestseller *Invisible Man, Got the Whole World Watching*. His work has appeared online and in print in the *New York Times*, *Washington Post*, *Harper's*, Artforum, Oxford American, *New Republic*, *GQ*, Complex, *Esquire*, *Playboy*, Bleacher Report, the *Nation*, the *Atlantic*, Pitchfork, Bookforum, and a number of other publications. He has appeared on *The Daily Show, PBS Newshour, Democracy Now!, Full Frontal with Samantha Bee*, MSNBC, CNN, NPR, and more national and local radio/television programs. He is featured in and was a consulting producer for "Rest in Power: The Trayvon Martin Story," the Paramount Network docuseries executive produced by Jay-Z. In 2014 and 2016, TheRoot .com named him one of the 100 Most Influential African Americans. He was also a 2017 NAACP Image Award Nominee. He is a fellow at Type Media Center. You can follow him on Twitter at @mychalsmith.